£1.49

7/16

The shortest possible game of chess

First published 1979
Fourth impression 1984
Second edition, revised 1990
All rights reserved

Published by
William Collins Sons and Company Limited,
Glasgow and London

© text 1979, 1989 W. T. McLeod and R. Mongredien
© illustrations 1979 Editions des deux Coqs d'Or, Paris

Printed and bound in Belgium by Proost International Book Production

ISBN (HB) 0 00 106252 2

ISBN (PB) 0 00 191223 2

BETTER CHESS
FOR YOUNG PLAYERS

William T. McLeod and Ronald Mongredien

Drawings by Jean-Paul Colbus

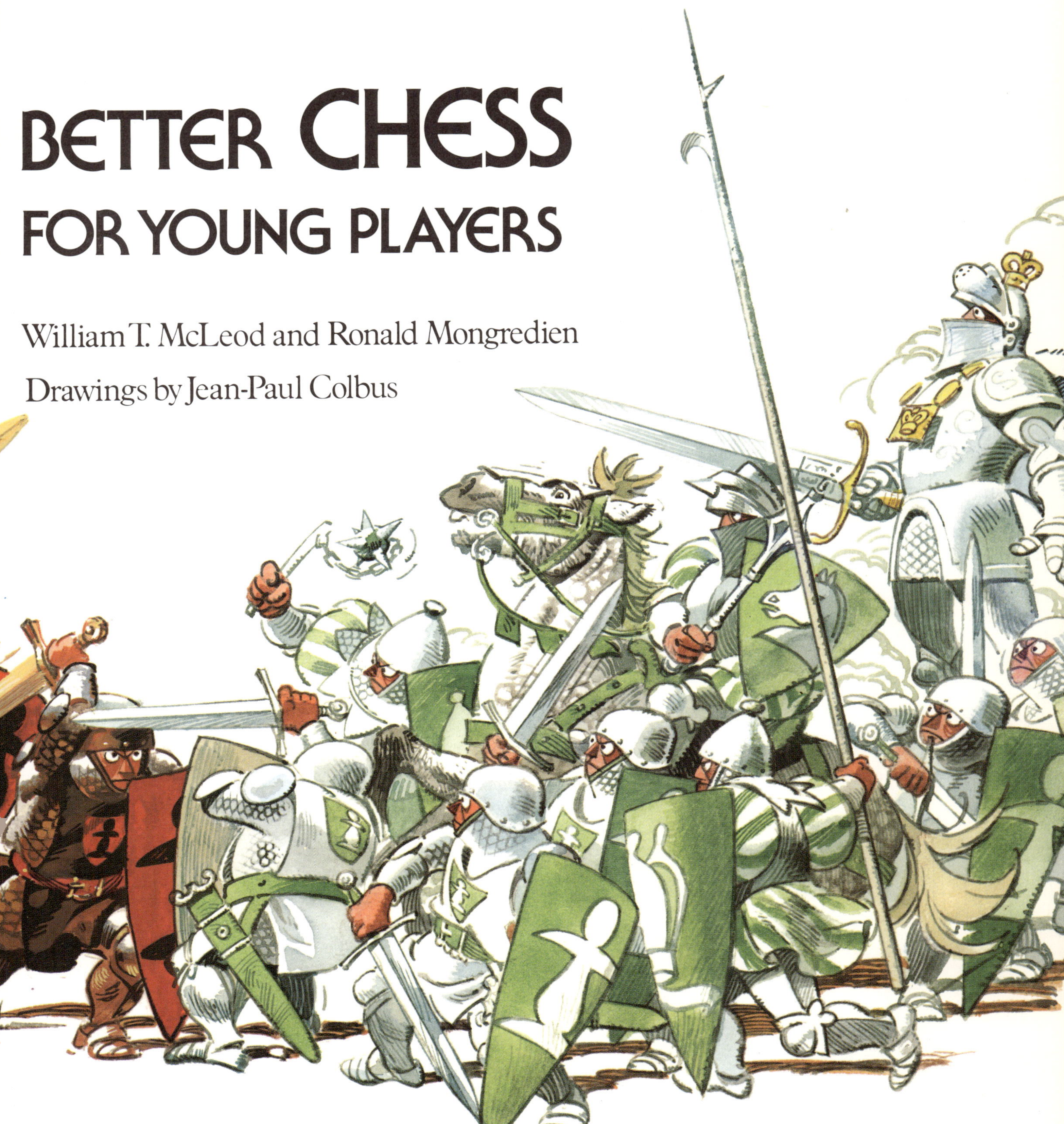

COLLINS

Glasgow and London

Contents

About this book

Chess is a great game—one of the greatest and oldest in the world. It has had a long and noble history from its origin in India some 1500 years ago. It has been the favourite game of emperors and kings, popes and bishops, powerful lords—and ladies, too—bankers, bandits, and ordinary people like us. Thousands of books have been written about how to play it.

In spite of all this, there is nothing to be nervous about. The only sensible reason for us to play chess is because we ENJOY it. Of course, it is not easy to enjoy a game if you nearly always lose.

This book will help you to enjoy chess more by helping you to play better and win more games. And the better you play, the more you enjoy the game, even when you don't win!

We would like you to read this book quite slowly, with your chess set beside you all the time. Every time you come to something new, set up the position on your board and try to understand the point or answer the question before going on. Even very clever people can't understand *everything* all at once; so don't worry if you have to read some parts more than once. Just take it slowly and you will soon *really* understand more about chess.

The book begins at the point where you have learned the rules and can play a game. If you play chess and enjoy it and want to enjoy it even more, read on . . .

The Authors

DO...!

We start with two things you must remember to do every time you play chess

1. *DO remember your manners!* Chess is a game for *two* people, and there are some things you must not do, out of fairness to the other person.

* Do not touch any of your men before you move. One of the rules of chess says that if you touch a man you *must* move it (if this is possible). So think carefully first, without touching, and when you have made up your mind go straight to the man and move.

If you need to touch a man to set it properly on its square, you should give warning of what you are doing by saying "j'adoube" (say: "zhadoob"—it's French for "I touch"); or just say "I adjust."

* Never touch the board or put your fingers on a square to help you think. You must train yourself to work out your moves in your head.

* Do not fidget or do anything to distract your opponent when it is his turn to move. Don't take something out of your pocket and start playing with it, and never speak to your opponent or ask him a question while he is thinking. If you *must* move about, good chess manners allow you to get up quietly and walk around to stretch your muscles.

* Never take moves back and never ask to change a move

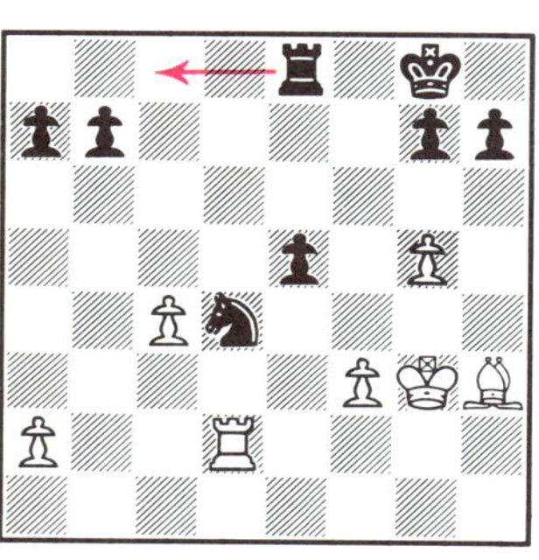

1. Black saw that White's c-pawn was unprotected, and quickly attacked it by moving Rc8. Why was this a blunder? **[A1]***

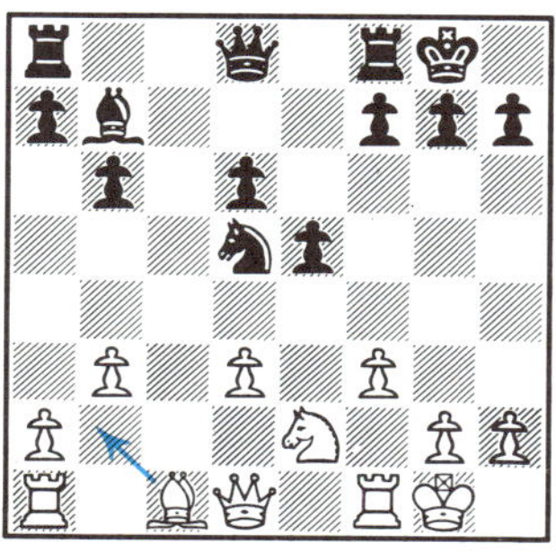

2. White moved his B as shown, to make way for his R on a1 (usually a sensible thing to do). Why was it a bad mistake this time? **[A2]**

3. White has left his N on its own far behind the enemy lines. Black can capture it in two moves. It is White to move. Can he save his N? **[A3]**

4. White has two rooks attacking Black's h-pawn. So Black plays Nf6 and has two pieces defending it. But White then plays Qd3. What can Black do? **[A4]**

5. White plays 1 h3. He does not see that his N is guarding an important square. 1 ... B×f3 2 Q×f3. How can Black win a piece? **[A5]**

6. Black plays Rd8, intending to play e5 next move. But this gives White the chance to play a deadly attacking move. What is it? **[A6]**

7. The black N is attacked by the white P and Black plays Na5. Why is this a blunder? What should he have played? **[A7]**

8. White thinks he can win a P for nothing and plays B×a7. He should have looked more carefully. Black can trap his B. How? **[A8]**

* *If you are not sure how to read and write chess moves, read pages 56 and 57 carefully before going any further.*

because "it's not what you really meant." Once a move is made it must stay made, even if it is a horrible blunder.

* Never show impatience, no matter how long your opponent takes to move. Sit quietly or, if you must, leave the board till your opponent has moved or—best of all—use the time to study the position some more and work out what is going to happen.

* Never complain or make excuses when you lose. Nobody likes a bad loser. This does not mean that you should not try to find out *why* you lost—talking about *that* with your opponent could help you to play better next time.

The second thing you must remember always is . . .

2. *DO look after your men*

You must learn to look after your men, and this means *all* your men, *all* the time. It is fatally easy to lose a piece for nothing as a result of a moment's carelessness, either by moving it to a square on which it can be captured or failing to see that a piece is being attacked.

Here are some simple rules that will help you to avoid such disasters. If you can remember the following *every* time you move and every time your opponent moves, you will not lose a piece for nothing.

* *Don't move into danger*

It seems easy to avoid moving a piece on to a square that is protected by an enemy pawn or piece, but it is surprisingly easy to blunder in this way when you are thinking hard about something else. See Diagram 1.

Sometimes, however, the danger is not so obvious. Do remember to make sure that your move does not give your opponent a chance to do something unexpected that loses you material the move *after* next. See Diagram 2.

* *Protect your men*

Protect your men at all times. This means not leaving a piece out on its own, even if it is not being attacked at the moment. Try to keep your knights, bishops, and rooks where they can be protected by pawns. See Diagram 3.

See that you have more men protecting a pawn or piece than your opponent has attacking it. See Diagram 4.

* *When a man is attacked, do something*

Some attacks are obvious and easily dealt with. But keep an eye open for the disguised or less obvious attack, especially for the deadly double attack. It is often too late to do anything once such an attack is made! You must try to see it *before* it happens! See Diagrams 5 and 6.

* *Don't let a piece be trapped*

First of all, don't walk into a trap. This means NEVER move a piece to a square from which it has no retreat square if it is attacked. See Diagram 7.

Next, don't let a trap be built around you. This means keeping *open lines* to allow other pieces to move up in support and watching that your opponent does not cut off your lines of retreat. See Diagram 8.

Know your pieces

When we talk of a "piece" in chess we mean any man that is not a pawn. A "man" can be either a pawn or a piece. We are speaking here of pieces. Pawns are so important that they will have pages to themselves later on in the book.

The chess pieces are not all equal in strength or equal in value. If you capture an enemy knight and lose your queen in exchange you have made a serious loss—so serious in fact that you will probably lose the game, unless your opponent also makes a mistake.

These two pages will tell you something about the value of the pieces and help you not to give up a valuable piece for one of less value. A single pawn is the least valuable man on the board, and chess players usually count the value of the pieces as the number of pawns each piece is worth.

1. *The Knight*
The knight is worth 3 pawns. As a knight is the only piece that can jump over a man, it is at its best on a crowded board. This means that it is especially valuable in the early stages of a game when both armies are still strong.

1. "Losing the exchange" (1). White to move. Why must Black lose the exchange (lose a R for a N)? What is White's move? **[A1]**

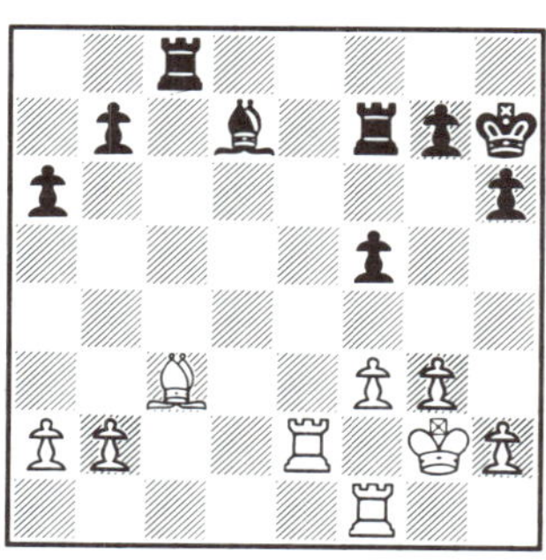

2. "Losing the exchange" (2). Black to move. How can he make sure of winning the exchange? (Clue: both white rooks stand on the same diagonal.) **[A2]**

3. Sometimes a N is less valuable than a P! For instance, in the position shown, 1 … N×c3 2 b×c3. Why must White now lose? **[A3]**

4. When is a R not worth 5 pawns? When it is up against two pawns on the sixth rank. It is White to move. Can the black R stop him queening one of his pawns? **[A4]**

5. Sometimes the mighty Q is worth less than a N. In this example White thinks all is well, but Black does not agree 1 … Q×c2! What happens next? **[A5]**

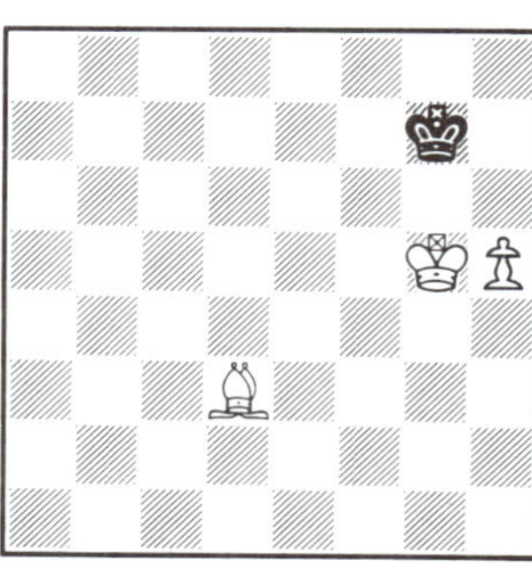

6. Sometimes a piece is worth nothing at all! Here is a tricky position. White is a B and P up, and his P is on the 5th rank. Can he win the game? Try it and see. **[A6]**

4. *The Queen*

The queen is worth 9 pawns (even though we only have 8 in our army!). She is by far the strongest piece on the board, being the equal of both bishops and a knight, or both knights and a bishop. She is worth one pawn more than a rook and a bishop, or a rook and a knight. But notice that she is not as valuable as 2 rooks—this can be especially true in the ending, when there are few men on the board.

2. *The Bishop*

The bishop is also worth 3 pawns. This means that a bishop and a knight are about equal in value. There are two other things to remember, however.

As bishops move in straight lines, they can become more valuable as the game goes on and they have long, empty diagonals to move along. Then they can get quickly from one side of the board to the other, attacking or supporting where most needed.

But a single bishop can cover only half the squares on the board, as it moves on light squares only *or* dark squares only. This means that *two* bishops between them cover all the squares, and for this reason most players try to keep both their bishops as long as possible. Near the end of a game, a player who still has both his bishops usually has an advantage over a player who has a bishop and a knight, even though each pair is worth 6 pawns.

3. *The Rook*

The rook is worth 5 pawns. This means that a rook is also worth a knight and 2 pawns or a bishop and 2 pawns. But a rook is worth *less* than 2 knights or 2 bishops, or a knight and a bishop.

Quite often a player is forced to give up a rook in exchange for a knight or a bishop. When he has to do this, he is said to have "lost the exchange," and he is usually at a disadvantage from then on. See Diagrams 1 and 2.

5. *The King*

The value of the king cannot be counted in number of pawns. If the king can be captured the game is over. The king is beyond price.

6. *Arithmetic is not always right!*

Please remember that the values of the pieces as just described can only be a *rough guide*. They are true only in equal or "normal" positions. But the position at any point in a game is often far from normal, and then these rough values are no longer true.

We finish this part with some examples to show you what we mean. See Diagrams 3–6.

Look before you leap!

1. White is sure he has found a way of capturing a P for nothing, and he plays Rd6, threatening two black pawns at the same time. What was his mistake? **[A1]**

2. White wants to stop Black from playing ... e5, attacking White's B and N. (Why can the white B not then take the black P?) So White plays e4. Is this sensible? **[A2]**

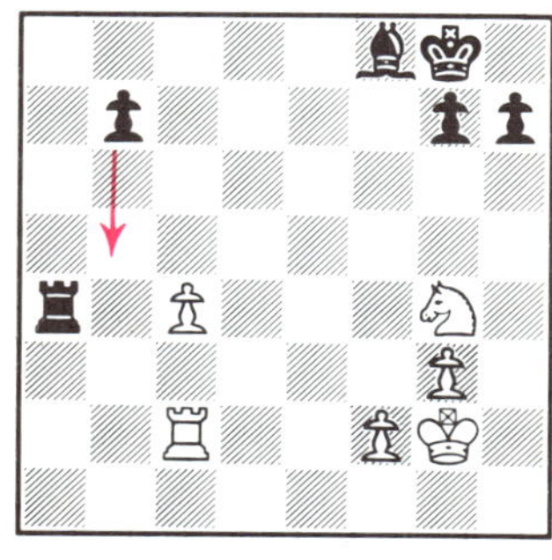

3. Black plays ... b5 and the white P is under attack from the black R and the black P, and is only protected once, by the white R. Should White just play c×b5? **[A3]**

The first step towards winning is to avoid losing. This page and the next three will help you not to lose. They list some simple secret questions that you should ask yourself EVERY time you move and EVERY time your opponent moves.

First of all, *before* every move you make, you should ask yourself three questions:

1. Can the man I move be captured or exchanged off?
2. Am I *exposing* one of my men to attack?
3. Am I lifting my guard over an important square or man?

Just three questions to answer —not too much to remember, is it? But the trick is to remember them EVERY move you make!

Here now are some examples of what we mean. Study each example carefully with your own board and men, so that you can be sure you know exactly what these three secret questions are about.

1. *Can the man I move be captured or exchanged off?*

For the moment we will think only about men that can be captured. Exchanging men in chess is so important that we shall leave it for some special pages later in the book.

Most players most of the time do not move a man on to a square on which he can be captured. When a blunder like this is made, it is sometimes just sheer carelessness; but more often it is because the player is thinking so hard about what he is trying to do that he doesn't notice an enemy man lying in ambush. For example, look at Diagram 1.

The way to avoid such disasters is simple. If you ask yourself this first question EVERY time you move, you should never again lose a man for nothing by moving him to a square that the enemy has guarded.

2. *Am I exposing one of my men to attack?*

This question means: is the man I am thinking of moving protecting another man from attack, so that after I move it the other man can be captured?

Look at Diagram 2 and you will see what we mean. *You* would not make a mistake if you were White, *if* you remembered to ask yourself our secret question. After you have answered the question under the diagram, look at the position again and see if you can find two other moves that White might make that would be wrong for the same kind of reason.

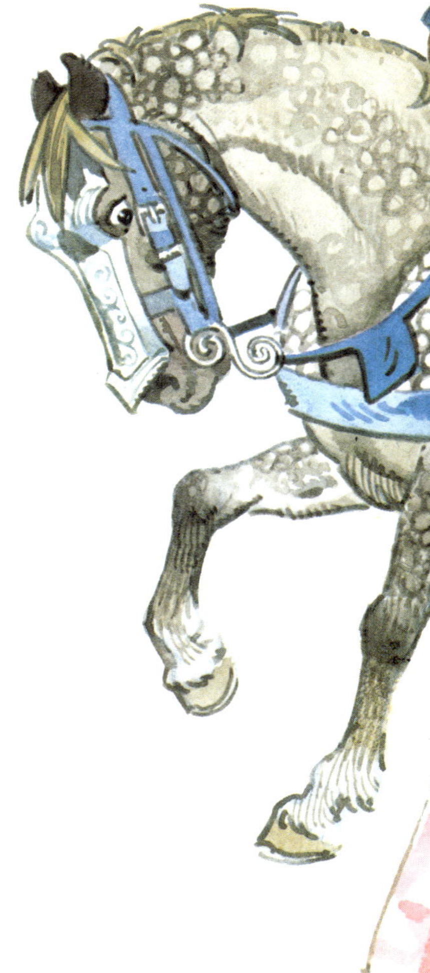

Study Diagrams 3 and 4 and you will see two other examples to help you understand how important this second secret question is. It is important because it is very easy to give away a piece if you don't remember to ask the question before *every* move you make.

3. *Am I lifting my guard over an important square or man?*

When one of your men has been on guard duty for some time, it is easy to forget that he is needed where he is, especially if you suddenly see a way of using him to attack or capture an enemy man. Look at Diagram 5 and you will see how important it is to make sure the man you move is not on essential guard duty.

We round off this section with a last puzzle for you in Diagram 6.

> Remember—before EVERY move you make, answer these:
> 1. Can my man be captured?
> 2. Am I exposing another man to attack?
> 3. Am I lifting my guard?

4. White had a good plan – drive away the black N with his e-pawn and mate with the Q on h7. So when Black played ... c5, he eagerly pressed on with e5. What went wrong? **[A4]**

5. Black plays ... Qb6+, hoping White will play d4. Why? (Clue: does the move free a square for Black to occupy?) What *should* White play? **[A5]**

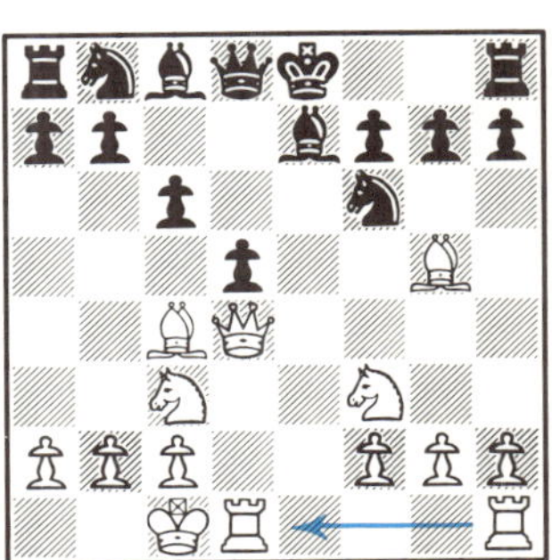

6. Black has just played ... d5, attacking the white B. White in reply plays R(h)e1. Has he not noticed the threat to his B? If you were Black would you snap up the B for nothing? **[A6]**

Watch the enemy

1. When White moved his B to d4, Black saw at once that his R was attacked by the white R. But his R is protected by his other R, so he looked to see if one of his other men was threatened. If so, what should he do about it? **[A1]**

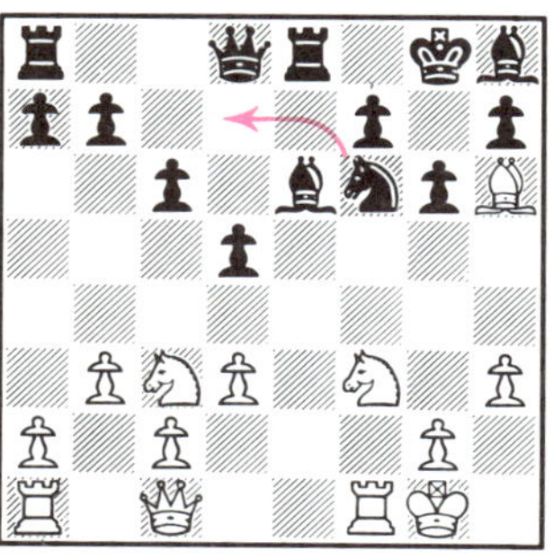

2. Black moves his N to d7. White asks himself: is it threatening one of my men? No. Has the move unmasked an attack on one of my men? Answer the question and say what you would do if you were White. **[A2]**

3. White moves his B to f1. Black asks: is it attacking one of my men? No. Has it unmasked an attack? No. So, where can it go next move? Well, where *can* it go, and should Black do something to stop it? **[A3]**

In chess it is just as important to think about enemy moves as it is to think about your own. So here are some more secret questions you must ask yourself, this time after EVERY enemy move.

1. Is one of my men attacked?
2. If not, why not?
   * Where is the enemy man going?
   * What square or squares is it covering?
3. Must I do something about it or can I just carry on with my plan?

Here are some examples to show how important these questions are.

1. *Is one of my men attacked?*
Remember that an attack can come from the man that has just moved or from a piece that the move has uncovered. Look at these examples (Diagrams 1 and 2).

2. *If not, where is the man going?*
If an enemy move does not attack one of your men, you must ask yourself whether the man that has moved is on its way somewhere. It could be making for a square that will cause you trouble *next move*. If so, you must do something before it gets there.

Study Diagrams 3 and 4 and you will see what we mean.

The enemy man could also be guarding or attacking an important *square*. Look at the example in Diagram 5.

3. *Must I do something about it or can I carry on with my plan?*
This is the most difficult of the questions to answer. Sometimes it is possible to ignore an enemy threat because your own attack will burst upon him first. Knowing when this is the case is a great part of the secret of winning at chess and you will learn more about this as you read the rest of the book.

In the meantime, here are two examples to be going on with (Diagrams 6 and 7).

A Warning!
If you are attacking hard and your opponent has to play a defensive move, you must *still* ask your secret questions after his move. Otherwise you could get a nasty surprise. Look at Diagram 8.

Remember—
Before every move you make:
1. Can my man be captured?
2. Am I exposing a man to attack?
3. Am I lifting my guard?

After every move your opponent makes:
1. Is one of my men attacked?
2. Where is the enemy man going?
3. Must I do something about it?

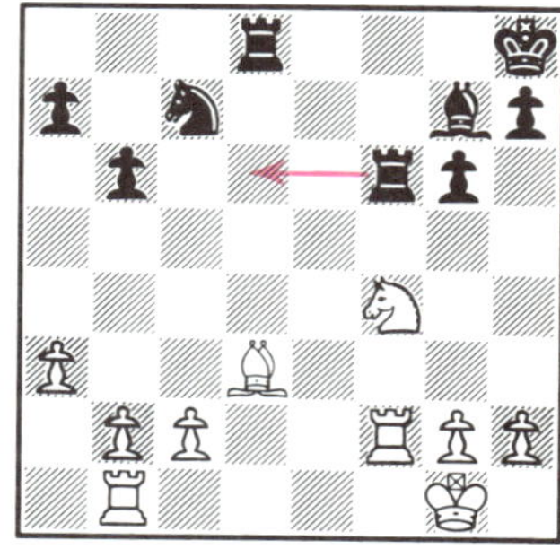

4. Black moves R(f)d6. The white B is attacked twice but is protected by a P and N and so looks safe. The unmasked B attacks White's b-pawn, but it too is protected. Is there any other danger and if so what should White do? **[A4]**

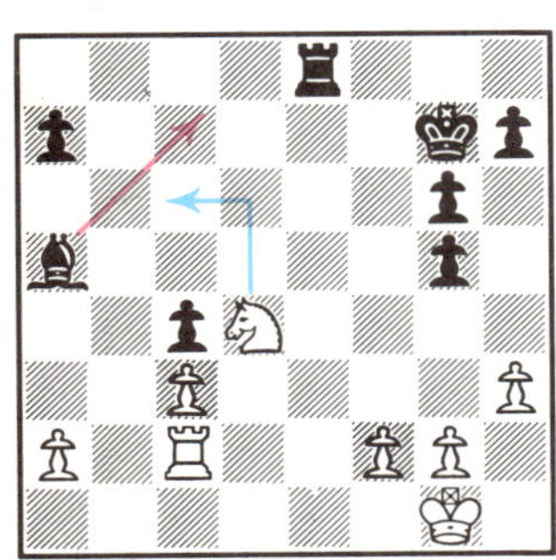

5. White has moved his N to c6 attacking the black B and a black P at the same time. In reply, Black moves his B to c7. He could have protected his P with his B. Ask yourself White's questions and say what you would do. **[A5]**

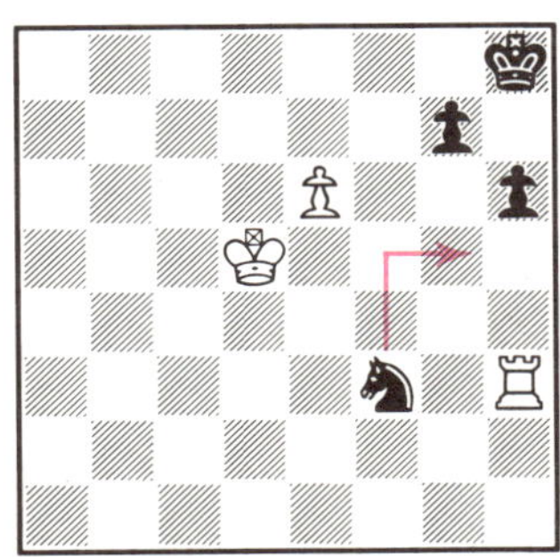

6. Black moves his N to g5, attacking the white R. Should White do something about this attack or can he just ignore it? This is quite tricky, so look at the position carefully and try to work out in your head what might happen. **[A6]**

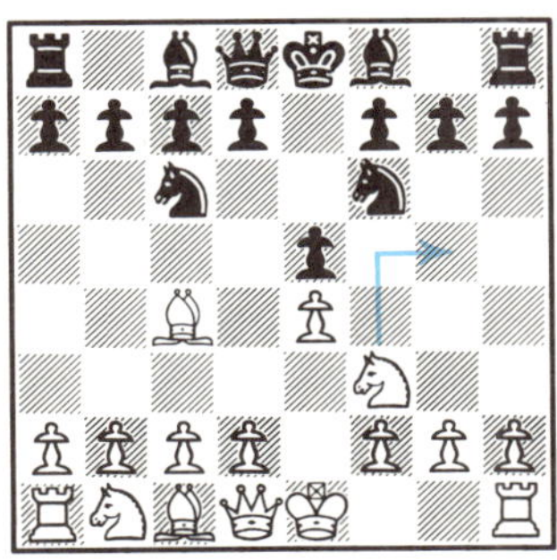

7. White's attack has come early in the game. With the move Ng5 he has two pieces attacking Black's f-pawn. Black *must* do something about it. Why? Can you see a move for Black that will stop White's attack? **[A7]**

8. Black moves his Q to c5, attacking White's c-pawn with two pieces. White defends his P with Qd3. Black sees that the white Q is threatening his a-pawn. He decides he can ignore this (why?) and press on with... d4. Was he right? **[A8]**

Begin like this

The shortest possible game of chess is mate in two moves by Black, like this (Diagram 1) – 1 f3 e5 2 g4 Qh4 mate.

Though no one would be silly enough to play like that, there are other quick mates to be avoided. For example (Diagram 2) 1 e4 e5 2 Bc4 a6 3 Qf3 b5 4 Q×f7 mate.

The most interesting thing about this mate is how easily Black could have prevented it. Even after White's third move, 3 Qf3, he could have played 3 ... Nf6, and this would have stopped any hope of a quick mate by White.

If both sides play sensibly there is no chance of winning in a few moves. Therefore, from the very beginning a good player prepares for a long struggle—not a single battle but a whole war.

In the opening (the first part of the game) each player should try to get his men into good positions so that they are ready both to attack and defend as soon as they are needed.

Here is a list of the things each player is trying to do in the opening. You need not learn this list off by heart, but read it carefully. You will come across the words it uses many times in the rest of this book and you will see bit by bit all that they mean.

* Get your pieces on to squares on which they can join in the fight. This is called "developing" your pieces.
* Bring out your knights and bishops so that they can get at the enemy.
* Keep your rooks and queen in reserve.
* Try to get control of the centre of the board.
* Keep a barricade in front of your king to protect him. Be especially careful about your f2, or f7, square, which in the early part of the game is protected only by the king.
* Try to keep your back rank free for your rooks to move along as they wish.

Now for some simple rules for you to follow, whether you are White or Black. There are dozens of ways of beginning a game of chess and no one "right" way. But if you follow these rules you will get a sensible position that will serve you well until you can do better for yourself.

How to begin

1. Move your e-pawn two squares. If you are Black you may have to choose your d-pawn, depending on White's first move.
2. Bring out a knight next and a bishop soon afterwards.
3. Bring out your K-side N and B and castle early.
4. Leave the pawns in front of your castled king, as a shield for him.
5. Try not to move the same piece twice in the opening – this wastes precious time.
6. Don't block your men – especially do not put a bishop on d3 or e3 before you have moved your d-pawn or e-pawn. You will just have to waste a move later on "unblocking" the pawn.
7. Try to have your rooks free to move along the back rank.
8. Don't push your pawns too far ahead too soon. Any one of them could become a queen, so they must *all* be looked after and protected.

Here to finish this part, is a game for you to play over. It shows some of these rules in action. You can learn quite a lot from it if you can see how White played the opening badly and how Black took advantage of this.

White	*Black*
1 Nf3	d5
2 c4	c6
3 c×d5	c×d5
4 d4	Nf6
5 Nc3	Nc6
6 Ne5	

Too soon, moving the same piece twice before developing a B and castling.

6 …	e6

1. The shortest possible game of chess.

2. Don't fall for this quick mate!

7 N×c6
Exchanging off his one active piece and making Black's centre pawns stronger.
7 …   b×c6
8 Bg5   Qb6
Attacking White's b-pawn and occupying the half-open b-file.
9 Qd2   Rb8
Attacking the b-pawn once again.
10 B×f6   g×f6
11 O–O–O
Mistakenly castling "into" Black's attack.
11 …   Qa5
12 Qc2   Ba3!
A nasty surprise for White. 13 b×a3 loses the Q and a P for a B and R, and lays White's K bare. Try it and see.

13 Na4
Trying to cut the B off from the Q.
13 …   Rb4
Threatening the N and tempting the white Q away from the scene of the action.
14 Q×c6+   Bd7
At this point White resigned.

The game might have finished like this: 15 Qa8+ Ke7 16 Q×h8 Rc4+ 17 Kb1 B×a4 18 Rc1 Qd2 19 R×c4 Q×b2 mate.

If 15 Qc3, then 15 … Rc4, and White must lose his Q for a R. 16 Q×c4 d×c4 17 b×a3 B×a4 18 Rd2 Qc3+ 19 Kb1 Q×d2, and White's position is hopeless.

An opening examined

In these two pages we examine a well-known opening. It is called the Ruy Lopez opening, after the Spanish priest who described it in the 16th century. It is still one of the best openings today. We try to explain some of the reasons for each move to help you to think about your own moves when you are playing.

White	*Black*
1 e4	e5

Both players claim some ground in the centre and open up paths for their K-side bishops.

2 Nf3

White develops a piece *and* attacks Black's e-pawn.

2 … Nc6

Black defends his pawn *and* develops a piece.

3 Bb5

White clears the way for castling and develops a piece.

3 … a6

Black makes White spend a move rescuing his bishop and at the same time prepares for … b5 later, claiming space on the queen's side.

4 Ba4

White keeps his bishop in line with Black's king, so that if Black moves his d-pawn, the N on c6 will be unable to move to defend the e-pawn.

4 … Nf6

Black develops another piece and threatens White's KP.

5 O–O

White ignores the threat to his e-pawn and castles.

5 … Be7

Black prefers to leave White's e-pawn and clear the way for castling.

6 Re1

White supports his e-pawn. (He intends to play c3 and then d4.)

6 … b5

Now that Black's king's side is developed he can take time to drive White's bishop away and start expanding on the queen's side (before White can play c3, giving his bishop a safe refuge on c2).

7 Bb3 d6

Now Black can support his e-pawn with a pawn and open a path for his B on c8.

8 c3

Still preparing for d4.

8 … O–O

Black takes advantage of the lull to get his king to safety.

9 h3

White wants to stop Black playing Bg4, because this would stop the white N from covering the d4 square (because of the threat to the white queen).

9 … Na5

Black wants to go ahead with his expansion on the queen's side by playing … c5, so he gets his knight out of the way and in the same move threatens to exchange White's useful B on b3, knowing that White will take a move to rescue it once again. But Black will sooner or later have to take a move to bring his N back from the edge of the board and into the fight.

10 Bc2 c5

Black goes on with his queen-side plan and gets another man covering the key square, d4 (to which White wishes to advance his d-pawn).

11 d4

The advance which White has been preparing in order to threaten Black's e-pawn and open up the centre.

11 … Qc7

Black defends his e-pawn and helps to free his back rank for his rooks.

The opening is now over, and both players are free to plan for the middle game. White usually tries to attack on the king's side. To help him he often brings his Q-side N over to the K-side, by way of d2, f1, and g3 or e3. Black has a chance on the queen's side but must get his N on a5 back into play and develop his Q-side B so that his rooks are united. He will probably want a rook on d8, since the d-file will be opened before long. It's often a good idea to place one of your rooks opposite the enemy queen.

The game we have been studying is an example of the "closed" Ruy Lopez. It is "closed" because the centre remains closed throughout the opening – that is the pawns remain on the e-file and d-file. If Black captures White's e-pawn on his fifth move, the game becomes an "open" Ruy Lopez. Let us look at what might happen.

White	*Black*
1 e4	e5
2 Nf3	Nc6
3 Bb5	a6
4 Ba4	Nf6
5 O–O	N×e4

Black decides to open the centre. Note that Black should not try to hold on to his pawn lead. Note also that Black has moved a piece twice in the opening. This should give White a very small lead in development.

6 d4

Black cannot capture this pawn without getting his N into trouble, after 7 Re1. White is a little better developed than Black, so he decides to open up the centre completely, to allow his pieces free play.

6 … b5

Black wants to play … d5 but decides he must get the white B off the same diagonal as his K, or else his N on c6 would not be able to move once the d-pawn had advanced.

7 Bb3	d5
8 d×e5	Be6

Black has to defend his d-pawn a second time.

9 Qe2

Giving his rook more freedom.

9 … Be7

Black decides to continue his development and prepares to castle.

10 Rd1

This time it is White who places a rook opposite the enemy Q.

10 ... O–O

Black has only one pawn really guarding c4, since the d-pawn cannot leave the d-file because of R×d8. White takes advantage of this.

11 c4 b×c4

Black cannot allow his d-pawn to be captured as the white d-pawn will then be attacking a B and N at the same time and Black will lose a piece.

12 B×c4 Qd7

Black unites his rooks.

13 Nc3

White could win a pawn (13 B×a3) but this allows Black to counterattack with 13 ... Nc5, after which the open a- and b- files could be to Black's advantage. So White prefers to bring another piece into play.

13 ... N×c3

Forced, because the d-pawn is still stuck on the d-file and not really defending the black N at all.

14 b×c3 f6

Getting rid of White's dangerous e-pawn.

15 e×f6 B×f6

Again, the opening is over and the position is almost equal. But many experts think that White has slightly better attacking chances. Two good moves for White are 16 Bg5 and 16 Ng5.

On balance, it is better for Black to choose the first version of the Ruy Lopez.

Perhaps the most important lesson of all to learn here, is that no move is made in chess without first looking at the move your opponent has just made and finding out what he is up to, for only then can you think out and play the best possible move in reply. You will not be able to do this every time at first. But if you keep asking our questions at every move, you will get better at it and find yourself beating players who used to beat you.

1. The position after 11 moves. Look at it carefully and make sure you understand the moves leading up to it.

2. The position after 15 moves. White has opened up the centre to give his pieces more freedom.

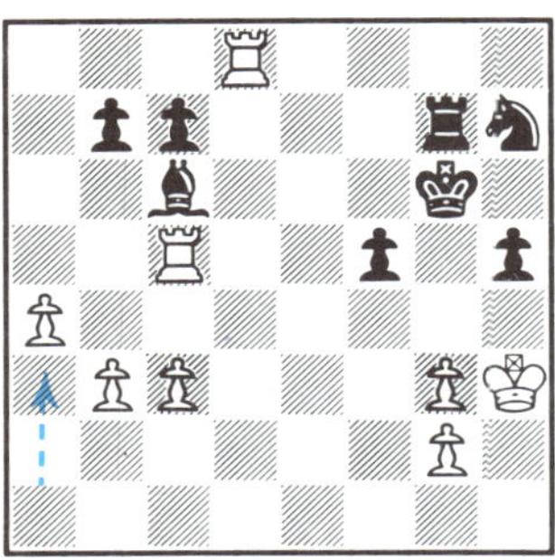

1. White's plan was to queen one of his Q-side pawns, so he played 1 a4, paying no heed to the black N right on the other side of the board. So: 1 ... Ng5+ 2 Kh2 Ne6, and now White must lose the exchange: 3 R×c6 b×c6.

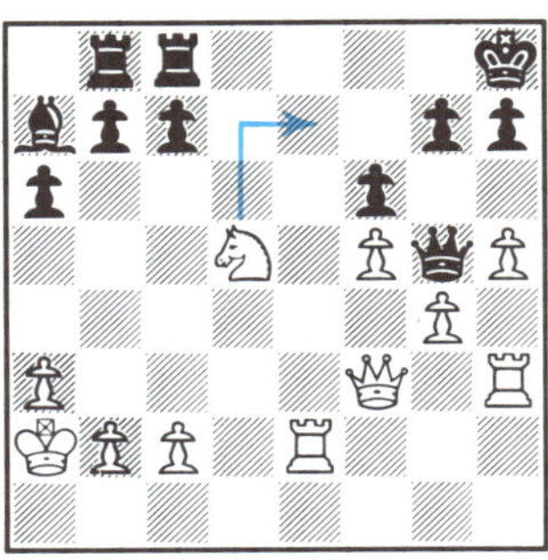

2. 1 Ne7 Rd8 2 Ng6+. (Only a N could squeeze into a square like that.) Now Black can move his K or take the N with his P. In either case, White has a certain mate in a few moves. Can you work out the moves in each case? **[A1]**

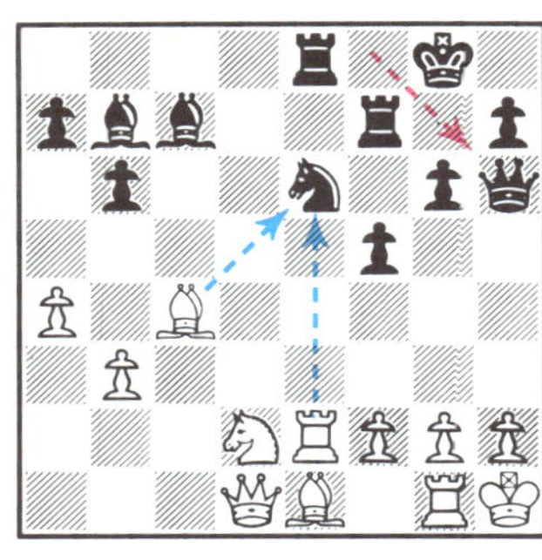

3. Black ignores the double attack on his N and moves ... Qh6, threatening mate next move. (How?) White cannot reply g3. (Why?) h3 still leads to mate next move. (How?) Has White lost the game? **[A2]**

4. On page 8 we saw how easily a N could be trapped at the side of the board. This is so important that here is another example. The N cannot move without being captured. White's next move should be obvious to you. **[A3]**

5. Yet another example as a warning never to put your N on a square from which it cannot escape. Black sees a chance to snatch a P and takes it without looking carefully enough. 1 ... N×a3. How can White trap the N? **[A4]**

6. White's N is very strongly placed. It covers a very important square (g7) and it cannot be forced to move. But there is also a very good outpost for the black N to occupy if he can. Can you spot it? **[A5]**

1. *A master of surprise*
Because of its jumping ability, the knight is the best guerilla fighter on the board. It can dart in from an unexpected direction and do great damage. It is an expert at the surprise attack. See Diagram 1. Always check where enemy knights can go next.

Use your Knights well

2. *It cannot be blocked*
Other men are no barrier to the knight. It can squeeze into tight spots, both to attack and defend, in a way that other pieces cannot, not even the powerful queen. Study Diagrams 2 and 3 for examples. Look out for chances to use your knights like this.

3. *It is strongest in the centre*
In the centre of the board, the knight *always* covers 8 squares, even if the board is crowded. The number of squares the other pieces can cover depend on how many men are in their path. Not so with the knight—it always has its 8 squares in view.

4. *But it can be trapped!*
Try to keep your knights away from the edge of the board. Of course, sometimes there is a good reason for moving a knight to the side of the board, but do not *leave* it there longer than you must. There are two reasons for this.

(i) At the edge of the board the knight covers only 4 squares and so it is only half as strong as it should be.
(ii) It is more easily trapped at the edge of the board—look at Diagrams 4 and 5.

Be on the lookout, so that your knights are not trapped. If you see that an enemy knight has only one or perhaps two squares to move to, it might be worthwhile to try to trap it.

5. *Knight outposts*
A knight is especially useful in the middle game if you make it an advanced strongpoint from which it cannot be made to retreat. It needs to be on a square on which it cannot be attacked by a P or exchanged off for an enemy B. Diagram 6 shows what is meant by a knight outpost.

Be on the lookout for a chance to set up a strong knight outpost, and don't let your opponent get a knight firmly settled in *your* camp.

6. *A sample game*
Here, to end this part, is a short game for you to play over and enjoy. Notice the part the knights play.

White	*Black*
1 e4	e5
2 Nf3	d6
3 Bc4	h6

Wanting to stop White from playing 4 Ng5

4 Nc3	Bg4

It is usually better to bring out at least one N first.

5 N×e5	B×d1
6 B×f7+	Ke2
7 Nd5 mate	

Use your Bishops well

1. *A long-range fighter*
Bishops are long-ranging pieces. They like open spaces and are strongest on long, clear diagonals. You should try to get your bishops firmly placed on long diagonals where they cannot be attacked by pawns or exchanged off for a knight. Best of all is to have both your bishops pointing at the enemy king. Look at Diagram 1. White's bishops are strong but Black's bishops are almost useless.

Look back to page 11 and read again what it says about bishops. You should note that one bishop cannot stop the enemy king crossing the board, but *two* bishops side by side can. Diagram 2 shows this in action.

2. *The fianchetto*
Because bishops can fire right across the board (if they are not blocked), they can help to control the centre without actually moving into it. This can leave the centre free for their pawns and protect the pawns from a distance, even from the edge of the board.

For this reason a player will sometimes develop one of his bishops to g2 (or g7) or b2 (or b7), from where it has a good view of one of the long diagonals. This is done by moving the g- or b-pawn one square and putting the bishop in its place. This move is called the "fianchetto" and a bishop developed like this is a fianchettoed bishop. See Diagrams 3, 4, and 5.

The word is Italian and comes from the Italian word for "flank" or "side", *fianco*. Italians say "fee-an-ket′to", but English-speaking chess players often say "fee-an-chet′o".

It is possible to fianchetto both bishops but this is not often done. The K-side B is fianchettoed more often than the Q-side B, for the fianchettoed K-side B is protected by the castled K and helps to keep the king's position strong. Black sometimes fianchettoes his Q-side B to attack White's e-pawn and his castled king's position.

3. *The "bad" bishop*
A bishop is "bad" when its path is blocked so that it cannot get into the game. Look at Diagram 6. Not only is White's B blocked but the pawns that are blocking it are also blocked. White simply cannot get his B into play, and this gives Black all the time in the world to plan a way to queen a pawn first and win.

Do not allow either of your bishops to become bad. Above all, do not block your bishop with your own pawns in the end game.

4. *A strong bishop*
Take good note of how a bishop and pawn can *support each other*. This is *not* true of a knight and a pawn. (Study Diagram 7.) A bishop and pawn supporting each other cannot be budged. Study Diagram 8. The white K will have plenty of time to come up and escort his P to its queening square.

5. *A tip for the end game!*
If your opponent has a single B in the end game, you should keep your pawns and pieces on squares of the *opposite* colour to the enemy bishop. If you do this, the bishop can *never* attack them. This applies especially to your K and your R (if you have one).

1. White's pieces are splendidly developed, while Black's have hardly any room to move. After 1 Nh5, White has a winning attack, thanks to his two powerful bishops. Finish the game for White.

2. The white P is only two squares away from queening and the black K is far away. Can the white K drive the bishops away and escort his P home before the black K arrives on the scene? Try it and see.

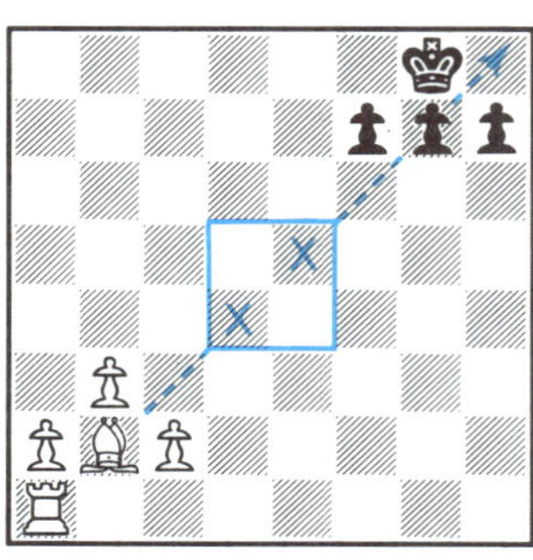

3. The Q-side fianchetto. See how it supports two important squares in the centre and protects the R. It is also a long-term threat to the enemy king's position. Often White protects his fianchettoed B by Rb1.

4. Black has fianchettoed his K-side B. It helps to protect his castled K, helps to control the central squares, and can threaten White's d-pawn and sometimes his R on a1, when the black N on f6 moves away.

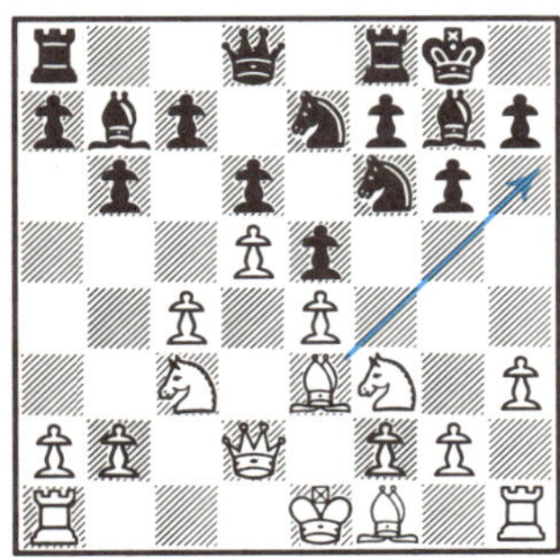

5. The fianchettoed B is so strong that the other player often tries to exchange it off. The diagram shows the usual way of doing this. When he sees this coming Black should move Re8 so that his B can retreat to h8.

6. An extreme example of a "bad" bishop in the end game. Notice that *all* White's men are on squares of the same colour as his B and *none* of Black's men are. Can Black take advantage of this to queen a P? **[A1]**

7. In this position the white K can attack the black P and the N can defend it. But watch: 1 Kh5 Nf7 2 Kg6 and now either the N or the P must fall next move.

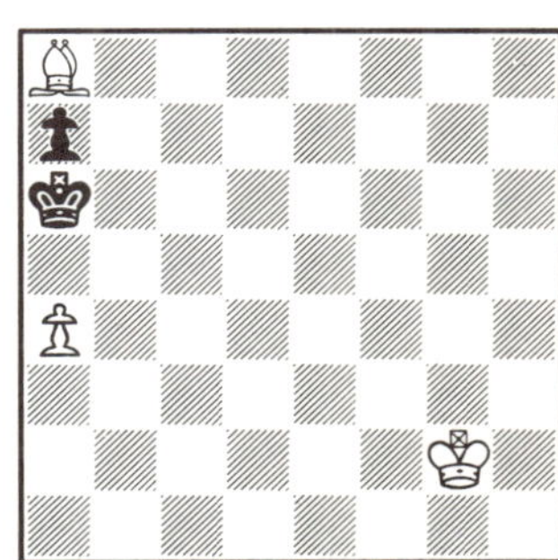

8. Here the black K can attack the white P and this time the white B can defend it. But there is a big difference. Can you see what it is and why it is important? **[A2]**

Use your Rooks well

1. *A long-range piece*
Like the bishop, the rook has long-range fire-power. It needs open files and ranks to move along in order to exert its full strength. Look at Diagram 1 and notice the difference between the white rooks and the black rooks. Try to position your rooks on open files so that they can fire into the enemy camp.

2. *Keep your rooks in reserve*
Do not bring your rooks out into the middle of the board too soon. Remember, it is particularly easy for a pawn to attack a rook and chase it away.

Do not bring your rooks into play by advancing your a- or h-pawn and moving your rook up behind it. Your first rook moves should usually be along the back rank to get them on to files on which they can protect your advanced pawns and pieces from behind.

Your K-side R should *usually* be brought towards the middle by castling. Turn back to pages 18 and 19 and look at how the rooks are handled.

3. *Do not expose an unprotected rook*
Have you noticed that at the beginning of the game rooks are the *only* pieces that are completely unprotected? They are *shielded* by the a- and b- and g- and h-pawns but there is no other piece protecting them. If you move the pawn shield, be extra careful not to expose an unprotected rook to attack. If you move the b- or g-pawn, make sure that an enemy bishop cannot threaten your rook, especially if it still cannot move. Look at Diagram 2.

Also, remember that you will sometimes be unable to capture with the a- or h-pawn if this will leave your rook exposed. Be careful not to be caught in this trap. Look at Diagram 3.

1. Black's rooks are not united and his B is hemmed in. His N has hardly any moves. White's rooks are beautifully placed on central files behind his dangerous advanced pawns. His B and N are ready for action.

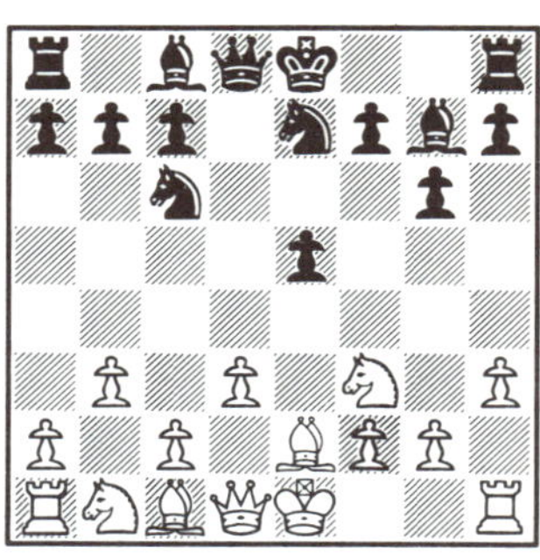

2. White wanted to fianchetto his Q-side B to pin Black's e-pawn where it was. So he played b3 intending Bb2 next move. But Black got in first. Can you find Black's move, and is there a way out for White? **[A1]**

3. Black thinks he can win a P. He plans the following moves: 1 … b5 2 a×b5 c×b5 3 Bd5 N(f)×d5 4 e×d5 f6 5 Bd2 Q×d5! A good effort! But this is what happened: 1 … b5 2 a×b5 c×b5 3 B×b5! Why is Black stuck? **[A2]**

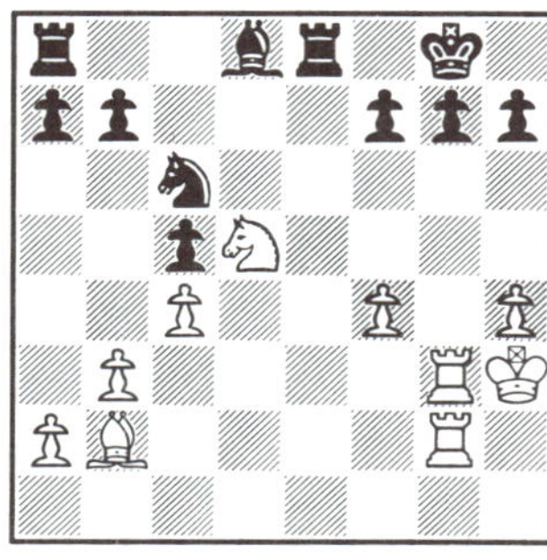

4. White's men are perfectly placed. His N is a strong outpost, his B is on a long open diagonal, and his doubled rooks threaten mate in two moves. If it is White to move he wins easily, but can you win for White if it is Black to move? **[A3]**

5. An example of how a rook on the 7th rank can be decisive. 1 Re7+ Kb8 2 Rf7. Now Black must lose his f-pawn, or, if he tries to use his R for counterattack, he will lose his g-pawn. Try both ways and see if you can win the game for White.

6. When Black attacks White's advanced P with 1 … Rh5, White's correct reply is to get his R behind his P to protect it: 2 Rc2. Now Black cannot stop him queening the P. If White's R is on the 6th, 7th, or 8th rank to begin with he cannot protect his P *and* queen it. Try it both ways and see for yourself.

4. *Unite your rooks*
Rooks are strongest when they protect each other. You should first try to get your rooks "united", that is, protecting each other along the back rank.

Next, as the game develops and the board becomes less crowded, try to get both your rooks supporting each other *on the same file*. This is called "doubling your rooks". Doubled rooks can be very strong. Study Diagram 4.

5. *A rook on the enemy's 2nd rank*
As the game moves towards the ending, if you can safely place one of your rooks on the enemy's 2nd rank, it can sometimes lead to mate or to winning a piece. Diagram 5 shows an example of this. A rook on the enemy's 2nd rank is *always* dangerous. Don't let it happen to you!

6. *The rook as a pawn escort*
The rook is extremely good at escorting a pawn to its queening square. So, if the result of a game depends on queening a pawn (as it often does), get your rook (or rooks, if you still have both) *behind* your best pawn (or pawns). Be ready to bring up your king in support, if necessary.

Remember that your rook is much more effective protecting your pawn from *behind*. If it is in front of your pawn, it must come off the all-important file to let the pawn through to queen, and when it does your pawn will be unprotected. Diagram 6 shows both these important points.

Here, to finish this section, is a fine example of how to use a pair of rooks so that each doubles the strength of the other. Black needed to win this game to win the competition. Can he do it? Set up the position shown on the left and play it through. We join the game near the end ....

White	*Black*
1 ...	Nf3+

Forcing White to exchange his B because of the threat to his R.

2 B×f3	g×f3
3 R×f3	R×a4

Opening the a-file for his rooks.

4 Rg8	Ra1
5 Rf8	R(e)a7

Ignoring the threat to his P and the trap of 5 ... Ke5 6 Rd8, followed by 7 Rd5 mate.

6 R×f6+	Ke7
7 Re6+	Kf7
8 Kc2	

White timed this just right, otherwise 8 ... R(2)a2 would have been mate.

8 ...	R(2)a2+
9 Kb3	Rg2
10 Rh6	R(a)a2

White should now have resigned but he played on to the bitter end: 11 Rh7+ Ke8 12 Rh8+ Kd7 13 Rh7+ Kc8 14 Rh8+ Kb7 15 Rh7+ Ka6, and there are no checks. 16 R×h5 R(g)b2 mate.

Use your Queen well

1. White has brought his Q out far too early to recapture a P. Black develops a N and threatens the white Q: 1 … Nc6 2 Qd3 Ne5 – again attacking the Q. 3 Qe3 Bc5 – the unhappy Q is attacked for a third time! 4 Qg3 B×f2+!! The Q is attacked yet again, so the B must be captured. Can you see what Black does next? **[A1]**

2. Can White take advantage of the position of Black's Q? Yes! 1 Nc4 and look how near the black Q is to being trapped. When it retreats, White uses his "free" move to get his N where he wants it. Can you see where? **[A2]**

3. The queen in attack! 1 … Qh1+ 2 Ke2 Qe4+ 3 Kf1 Rh1 mate. Try starting off with the positions of Black's Q and R reversed and you will see that there is no quick mate. That depended on the power of the Q to change direction.

4. The white N is attacked by three black pieces and cannot move because of the check from the black B. But it is defended by three pieces so all should be well. But is it? 1 … B×e4+ 2 R×e4 R×e4 3 Q×e4 R×e4 4 R×e4; and White is left with a R against Black's Q.

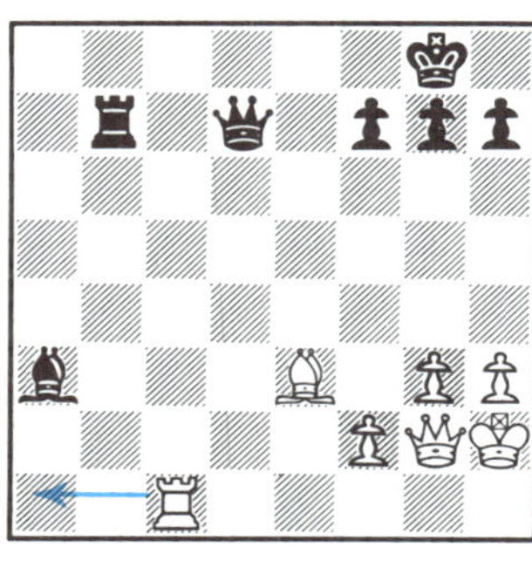

5. The black Q is defending her R from attack by the white Q. When White attacks the black B with his R as shown, Black moves his Q to e7 to defend the B as well. Is this sensible? **[A3]**

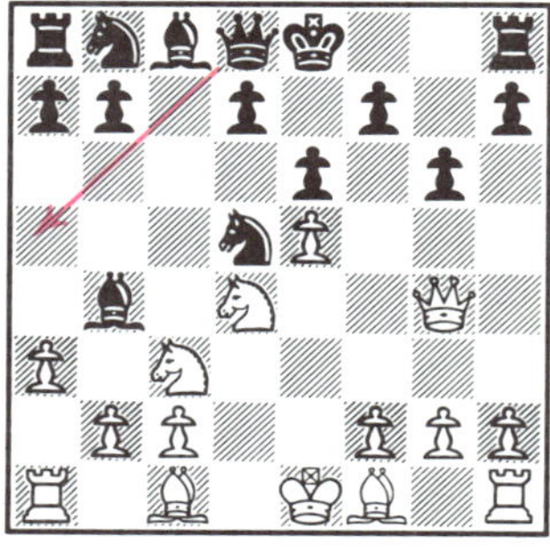

6. Black's B is attacked by the a-pawn. Black moves 1 … Qa5, thinking that if White's P took the B, he would capture the R on a1. This is what happened: 2 a×b4 Q×a1 3 Nb3! Trapped – and lost!

1. *The most powerful piece on the board*

The queen is the strongest and most valuable of your pieces. If you lose her by a blunder, you will usually lose the game too. So, the two first things to remember are:

* Do not bring your queen out too soon.
* Do not put her on a square where she can be easily attacked and driven about the board. Look at Diagram 1.

In the early part of the game keep your queen where she can retreat behind a shield of less valuable pieces.

2. *Do not be scared of the enemy queen*

Remember that the queen is so valuable that if she is attacked by any man, except the enemy queen, she is almost bound to retreat. A protected pawn is very good at annoying the mighty queen.

If the enemy queen comes out into the open board, attack her if you can do so safely without weakening your position. An attack on the enemy queen can give you a free move, so to speak. This is called "gaining a tempo". See Diagram 2.

3. *The queen is best in attack*

The queen's special power of moving like a rook and a bishop is seen at its best when she is attacking. This usually happens after the game has been going for some time. Diagram 3 shows an example of the queen's power in attack.

However, the queen is not so good in defence. If a man defended by the queen is attacked, the queen is sometimes too valuable to be used to recapture. (Diagram 4.)

Because the queen can move in any direction, it is dangerously easy to use her to defend two men at the same time. This can lead to disaster. Look at Diagram 5. Even the queen cannot be in two places at once!

Try not to allow your queen to be tied down to defending other pieces or pawns. Keep her free to move about the board and *attack*!

Though she can move in all directions, the queen can fall into a trap from which there is no escape. Look at Diagram 6 for an example. Be specially careful *every* time you move your queen.

4. *Beware the queen sacrifice!*

On page 21 you saw a game in which one player sacrificed his queen and won. Here is another, to warn you to look carefully for a trap before capturing a queen for nothing.

White	*Black*
1 e4	e5
2 Nf3	Nf6
3 N×e5	Nc6
4 N×c6	d×c6
5 d3	Bc5
6 Bg5	

White should play Be2.

6 …	N×e4
7 B×d8	B×f2+
8 Ke2	Bg4 mate

5. *The queen in action*

To end with here is an example of the queen in action from a game with a thrilling finish. Notice how she swoops about the board, attacking from all directions. Set up the position and play the end of the game over for yourself.

White	*Black*
1 Ng6+	h×g6
2 Qh4+	Kg8
3 f×g6	Ne7
4 Qh7+	Kf8
5 R×f6+	Ke8

The P cannot take the R because the queen will mate on f7.

6 Qh8+	Kd7

The Black K is seeking the safety of his queen's side corner, and White must stop this.

7 Qh3+	Kc6
8 b5+	K×b5

The K must keep off dark squares for fear of the deadly Be3+.

9 Qf1+	Kc6
10 Qc4+	Kd7
11 Qe6+	Ke8
12 Rf8+	K×f8
13 Qf7 mate	

Checkmate

When one of the two kings cannot immediately get out of check, it is CHECKMATE and the game is over. The first thing to notice about checkmate is that no man—not even the powerful queen—can give checkmate on its own. At least two men are needed to mate the enemy king. Of course the more men you have attacking the enemy king, the easier it is to mate him, especially if some of his own men are helping to block his escape.

This section looks at how to give checkmate with the *least* men, at the end of a game.

You can give checkmate

* with Q and K (or any other man)
* with R and K
* with two rooks
* with two bishops and K
* with B and N and K.

You cannot give checkmate

* with B and K
* with N and K or two knights and K.

1. *Practice with queen mates*

To mate with your queen and king (or other man), you should keep putting your queen a knight move away from the enemy king till you have driven him to the side of the board. Then you bring up your king or other man to cover the square in front of the enemy king and give checkmate on that square. Or you get your king in front of the enemy king so that he cannot leave the side of the board and give checkmate with the queen along the edge of the board.

Study Diagram 1 carefully, and then practise on the board for yourself until you are sure you know how to arrange checkmate with your queen and another man. Try using your queen and king first, then your queen and a bishop, and finally your queen and a knight.

2. *Practice with rook mates*

The position for mate with rook and king is shown in Diagram 2(B). It is the same as one of the standard queen checkmate positions, but it is a bit more difficult to drive the enemy king to the side of the board. You have to use your rook and king together to do this. This needs practice, so set up the board and keep on trying till you are sure you can do it every time. Now try Diagram 3.

Checkmate with two rooks (or rook and queen) is a little easier. You drive the enemy king to the edge of the board by checking him in a "leapfrog" way on each rank (or file) with each rook in turn. Diagram 2(A) should make this clear. When the enemy king reaches the edge of the board he has nowhere else to go and is mated.

1. **(A)** Checkmate with Q and K: you should aim for one of these positions. If the Q mates on f7, the white K can stand on e6, f6, or g6. If the Q mates from any of the marked squares along the back rank the white K must stand on f6. **(B)** Checkmate the Q and another man: the man, either P, B, N, or R, must cover the square in front of the K. With the R as shown, the Q could also mate on g1.

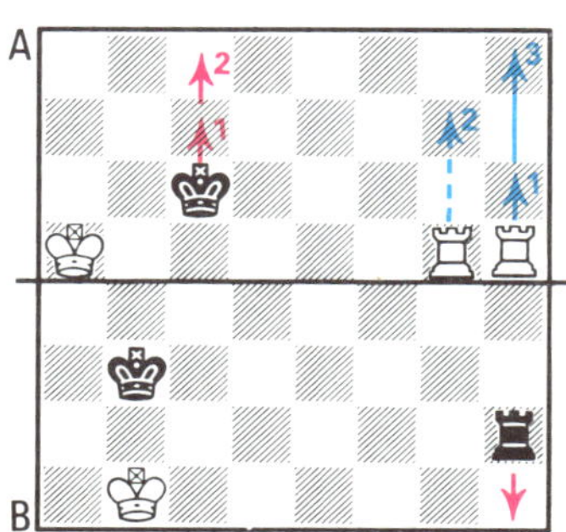

2. **(A)** Checkmate with two rooks. The black K is driven to the edge of the board: 1 Rh6+ Kc7 2 Rg7+ Kc8 3 Rh8 mate.
(B) Checkmate with R and K: the R keeps the white K on the back rank until the two kings are opposite one another and then mates with ... Rh1.

3. Practice: Set up the board as shown and see how many moves it takes you to deliver checkmate. Can you do it in 10 moves? Now put a white R in place of the Q and try again. Can you do it in 17 moves? **[A1]**

4. Black thinks he is safe from a back-rank mate because his Q guards his f8. White has a trick up his sleeve: 1 R×a6 b×a6 2 Qa8+ with mate next move. If Black refuses to capture the white R, it will checkmate him in two more moves.

3. *Back-rank mates*

One other kind of mate deserves special mention. "Back-rank mates" are important because it is *very* easy to be caught by one if you are not careful. Look at Diagrams 4 and 5.

When your castled king is behind its wall of three protecting pawns and the enemy rooks or queen are on open files, *always* be on your guard. Remember, too, that the queen can get to the back rank along a diagonal! If your opponent is threatening a back-rank mate it is best to put an end to the threat by moving one of the pawns in front of your king one square forward (usually the rook's pawn).

4. *Smothered mate*

A "smothered" mate happens when a king is completely hemmed in by his own men so that it cannot move and is then mated by an enemy knight. Diagram 6 shows what is meant. This kind of mate does not happen very often in actual games but it is a curiosity you should know about.

5. *Stalemate—a warning!*

When a player's king is not in check but his only possible moves when it is his turn would put his king into check, the position is *stalemate*. Neither side can win and the game is drawn. Look at Diagram 7 for two examples.

Many a player has been robbed of victory because he was too eager and did not see he had forced the enemy king into a stalemate position. Take care that you are not caught like this. Sometimes when you are losing it is possible to snatch a draw by playing for stalemate.

6. *Mate with minor pieces and king*

We have not talked about mates with two bishops and king or bishop and knight and king because they will seldom happen in your games. It is, however, excellent chess training to practise these mates. The positions to aim for are shown in Diagram 8. Set up your board and try each several times.

> Note: When a player has only his king left against a king and queen or king and rook it is usual for him to resign, as checkmate is only a matter of time. So these checkmates are seldom played out in actual games; but, of course, you have to know how to play them—just in case!

5. Here is another warning! 1 ... R×f2 2 R×f2 Rb1+ 3 Rf1 Bd4+ 4 Kh1 R×f1 mate.
Back-rank mates can come in many unexpected ways.

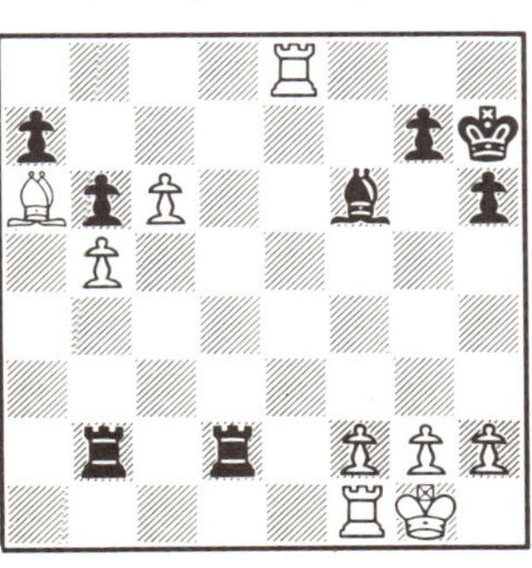

6. No hope of a back-rank mate for White with the black Q and two rooks guarding f8. But look! 1 Qa2+ Kh8 2 Nf7+ Kg8 3 Nh6 dbl ch Kh8 4 Qg8+ R×g8 5 Nf7 mate.

7. (**A**) Black has slipped in front of the white P and White has to stay next to it or lose it. He moves as shown. Stalemate! White has lost his win. (**B**) Black has been chasing the white K, keeping his Q a N-move away. But he does it once too often! Don't *you* be so eager. Always take care to leave the enemy K just enough room to move.

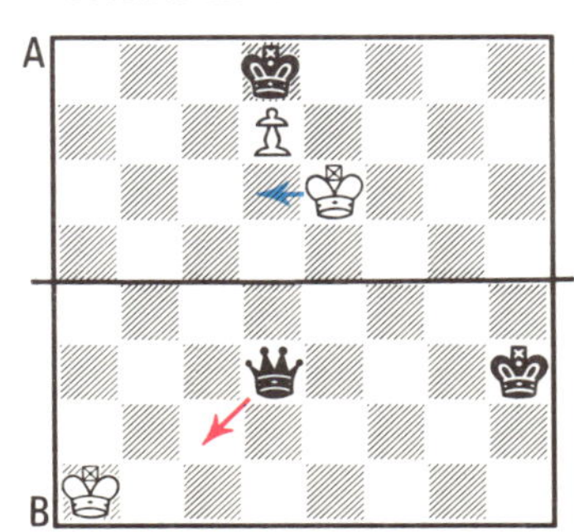

8. Checkmate with B, N and K, and with two bishops and K. The diagrams show the positions just before the final move in each case. Put the pieces anywhere on the board and see if you can checkmate the black K. **[A2]**

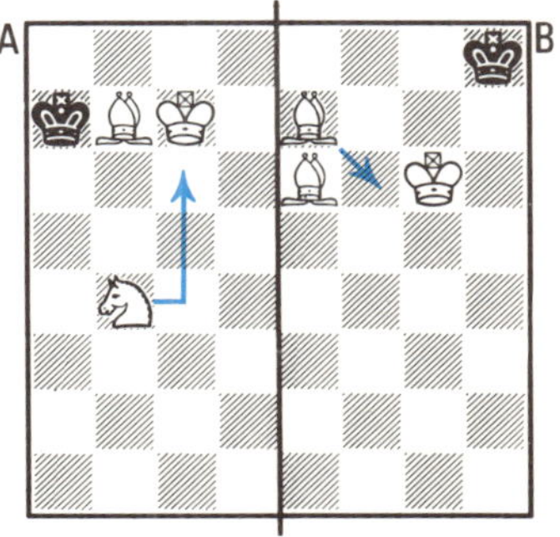

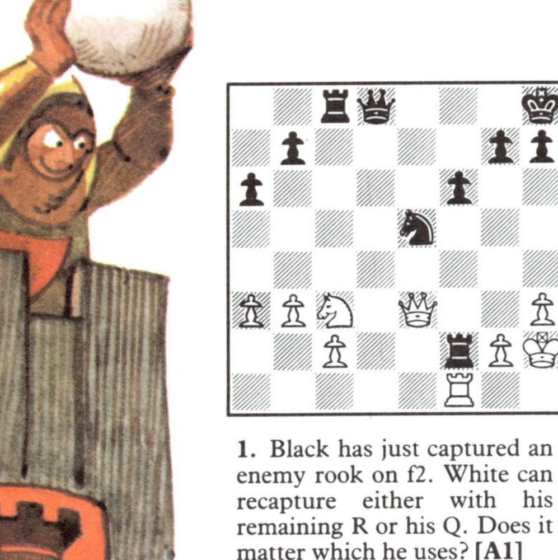

1. Black has just captured an enemy rook on f2. White can recapture either with his remaining R or his Q. Does it matter which he uses? **[A1]**

2. White has advanced a R into enemy territory and now finds that he has a R and a B under attack at the same time. Can he avoid losing a piece for nothing? **[A2]**

3. Black has a well-placed N in the centre of the board. White sees that he can exchange it off *and* lay a trap for Black. He plays 1 B×d5. What is the trap and how can Black avoid it? **[A3]**

4. Black's N is under attack, and he cannot move it because of Q×a8. He can protect his N in four ways (Bb7, Bd7, Qd7, Kd7). One of these moves is fatal to him. Which one? **[A4]**

Quizzes

Before we go on to the next part of the book, which will tell you about *tactics*, here are some quizzes to make sure you understand what you have read so far.

5. Black has moved 1 ... Ke7 to block the dangerous white P and attack it. White now plays 2 b4. No matter what Black had meant to do next, there is a move he should now make. What is it? **[A5]**

6. White has lost the exchange. But he saw a way of winning it back in two moves. What two moves did White plan? *Hint*: the N is a tricky customer – remember **[A6]**

7. Look carefully at this diagram. It is White to move. White thinks he has the better position. Is he right? He decides to attack. What should he do? *Hint*: look back at pages 24 and 25. **[A7]**

8. White has won a P and this can be very important in the end game. Black thinks he can win the P back and plays Rc3 attacking *two* white pawns. Must White lose one of them? **[A8]**

9. It is White to move. Here is your chance to win a game! White checkmated in five moves. Can you do the same? *Hint*: remember, pawns can become queens! **[A9]**

10. Both players have three pawns and a B (on different colours). White's e-pawn can take refuge from the enemy B on e3 and Black's g-pawn will be safe if it can reach g4. So, is the game a draw? White to move. **[A10]**

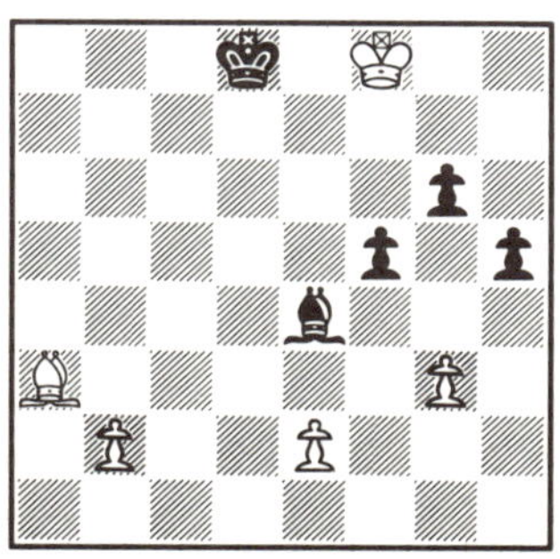

11. White has given up his Q in order to queen his c-pawn. But he is in check and his R is threatened. Can you find a move that will at least give him a chance to draw? **[A11]**

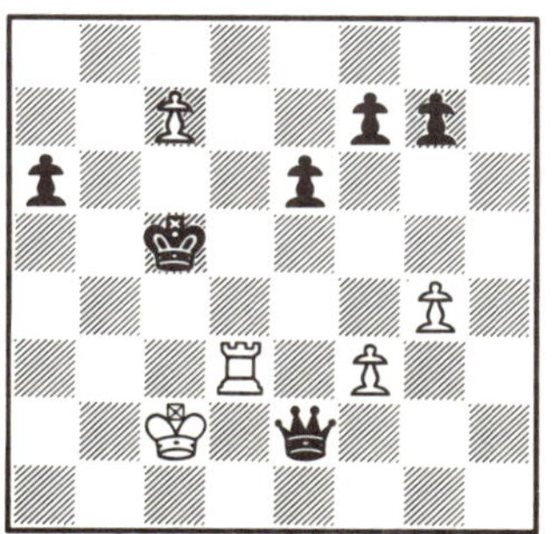

12. White is a P down and tried to win it back by 1 Nd4, hoping for 1 ... Q×b5 2 N×b5, when his N would be threatening Black's d-pawn and threatening to check on c7 and win the R on a8 next move. Can you find the unpleasant surprise Black sprang on him? **[A12]**

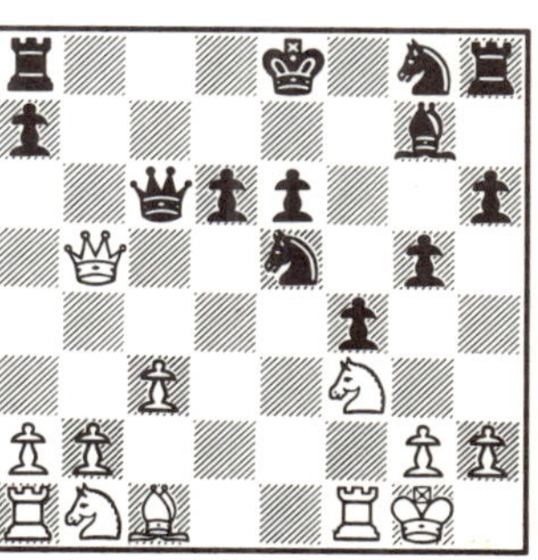

Forks

1. *What is a FORK?*
When a man attacks two enemy men at the same time, this is called a FORK. It is an attack with *two prongs*. If neither of the men that is attacked is protected, one of them is usually lost next move. Diagram 1 shows what can happen.

2. *Which men can fork?*
All men can fork, even the king and the pawn. Diagrams 2, 3, and 4 show how each of the men can fork. Study them carefully. You need to know all about forks.

3. *Forks are dangerous!*
You must beware of enemy forks. If you let yourself be forked you usually lose a man for nothing. At the same time, you must be able to spot chances to use forks yourself. The fork is one of the most important tricks in chess and you must master it.

After every enemy move, when you ask yourself what he is up to (remember pages 14–15?), you should add: "Can he fork me next move?" If the answer is "Yes", you should still be able to do something about it.

4. *Some tips about forks*
* Pawn forks happen more often in the early stages of a game, when the middle of the board is crowded. Diagram 5 shows what you must look out for.

In the later stages of a game, when the board is less crowded it is easier to see a pawn fork coming, and to avoid it. But this shows something else about this game of ours—sometimes a player makes a threat he knows his opponent will see because he knows his opponent will have to take avoiding action, and this gives the first player the chance to get on with what he really wants to do. A threatened pawn fork can be a very good example of this. Look at Diagram 6.

In chess, *the threat is sometimes stronger than the carrying out of the threat.*

* Rook forks are especially dangerous in the end game, when the

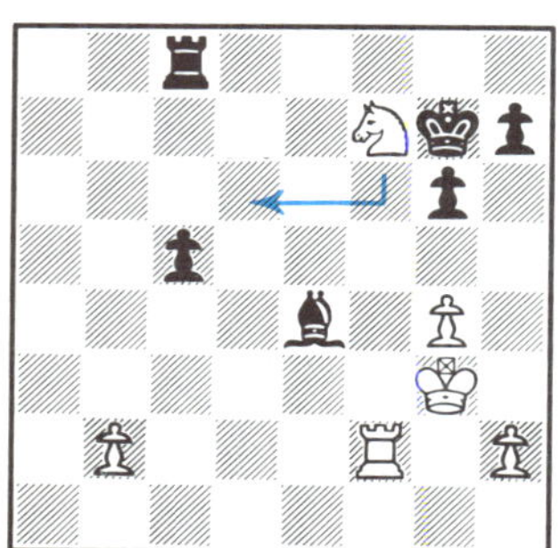

1. The white N moves as shown and forks Black's B and R. Black must lose one of his pieces for nothing.

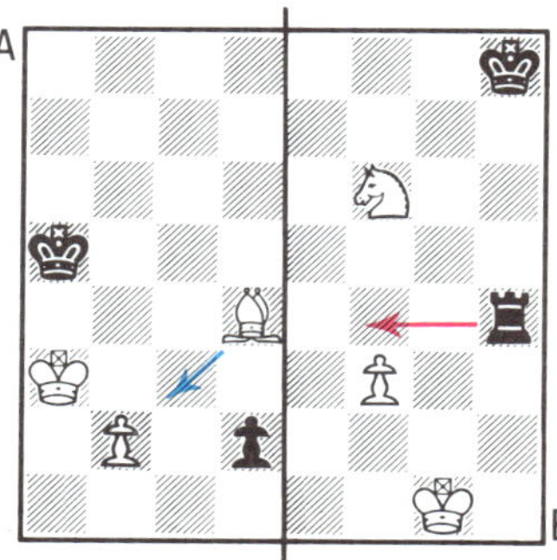

2. **(A)** The B fork wins Black's precious last P.
(B) The R fork wins White's P. Forks like these in the end game can decide the result of the game.

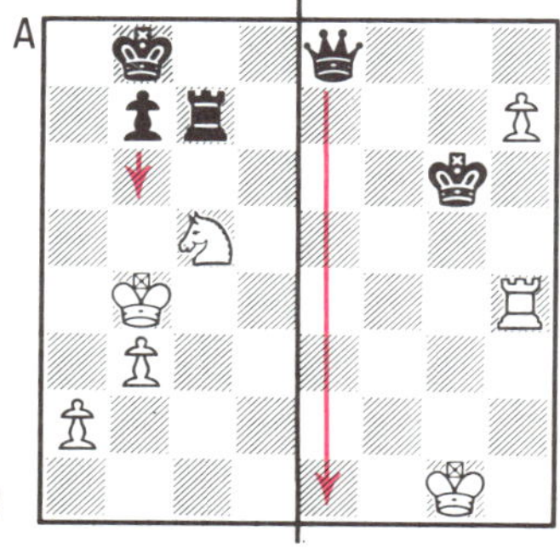

3. **(A)** Black moves b6. Was this sensible? **[A1]**
(B) The Q forks White's K and R.

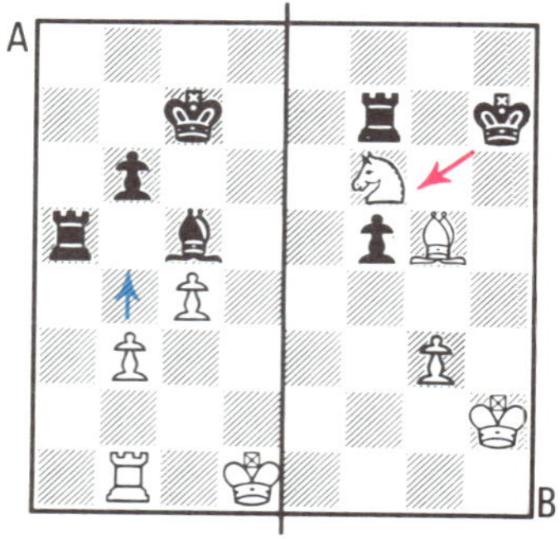

4. (A) A terrible blunder by Black allows White a P fork.
(B) A foolish check by the white N allows Black a K fork. Who should win? **[A2]**

queens are off the board. Open files and ranks make rook forks a real possibility—so be warned! Study Diagram 7.

★ In the end game, be careful not to fall for a king fork. It is very easy to forget that the king can attack. Look again at Diagram 4B on page 32.

Diagram 8 shows another example. Try to keep your men helping each other *from a distance* so that the enemy king has no chance of forking them.

5. *Knight forks*
Of all the men on the board the knight is by far the most dangerous forker. This is because the eight squares that it covers all lie in different directions. The queen and the rook can cover more squares but they run in straight lines and are easier to see. The twisting jumps of the knight allow it to make *unexpected* forks that can be very difficult to see before they happen. Look at Diagram 9!

ALWAYS keep a specially careful eye on the enemy knights, ALWAYS ask yourself what they are up to, ALWAYS make sure that one of them is not getting ready for a fork next move. Diagrams 10 and 11 show you how dangerous it can be to forget this.

6. *The invisible fork!*
Occasionally, a fork does not attack two enemy men, but one enemy man *and an important square*. We call this "the invisible fork" because it does not look like a fork at all. It can also be called a "feint attack" or pretend attack. When the enemy takes care of the man you are *pretending* to attack, you are free to occupy the key square that was your *real* intention. This is another example of a fake threat which you do not intend to carry out. It is made only to take your opponent's attention away from your true purpose. Diagram 12 shows the invisible fork in action. (Read again what we said about the *threat* of the pawn fork on page 32.)

7. *A last point*
A fork does not work if one of the two enemy men forked can move away *and* give check at the same time. Can you work out why?

> Forks are important! Always be on the lookout for them. Keep asking yourself:
> ★ Can my opponent fork me?
> ★ Can I fork him?

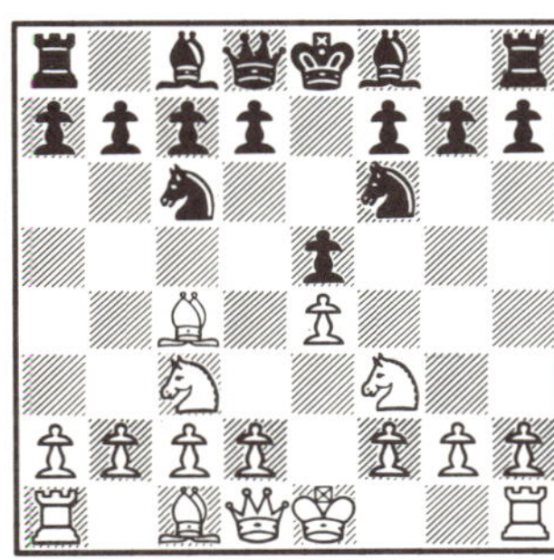

5. The "fork trick" in the opening: Black plays ... N×e4. Now, if White plays N×e4, Black replies ... d5, winning either the B or N in return. This breaks up White's strong centre.

6. 1 c5, threatening 2 c6, forking Black's R and Q. If Black attends to this threat, White has a surprise mate: 2 R×h7+ K×h7 3 Rh1 mate. If Black plays 1 ... Qc6 to stop the mate, then 2 Bd5 wins the exchange for White.

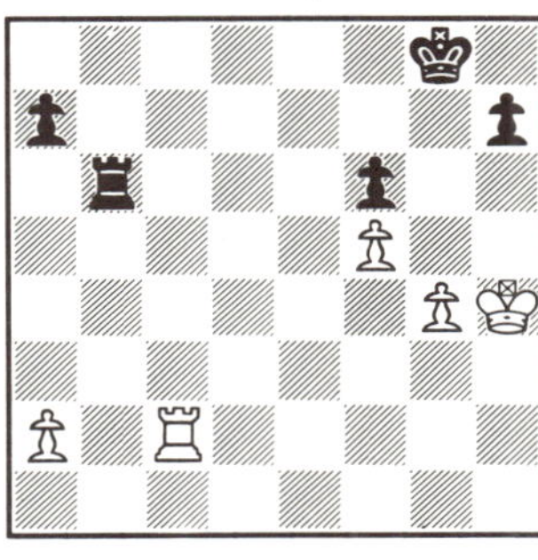

7. White plays 1 Rc8+, Kg7 2 Rc7+, winning the a-pawn. One way to avoid this kind of danger is to keep a R on your second rank to stop an enemy R settling there.

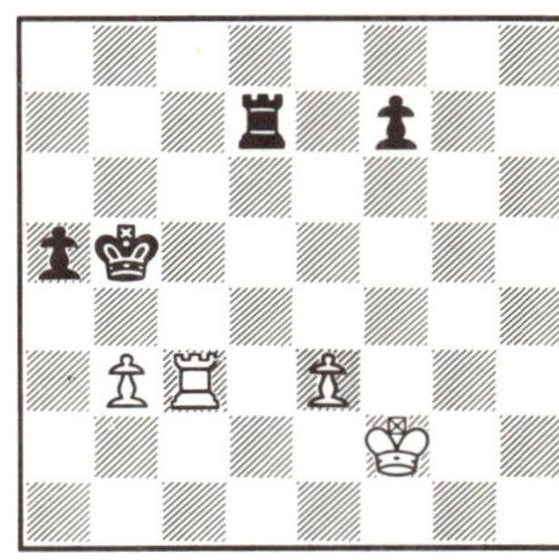

8. Another example of how dangerous the enemy K can be if you are careless. 1 ... Kb4 wins the b-pawn. Black should now easily queen the a-pawn and win.

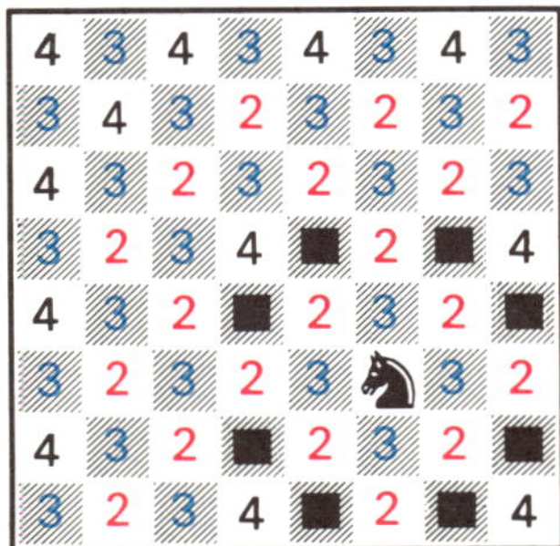

9. If a N is at least 2 squares away from the edge of the board, it can reach any square on the board in 4 moves. The diagram shows the squares a N on f3 can cover in 1,2,3 and 4 moves. No wonder the N is such a tricky customer!

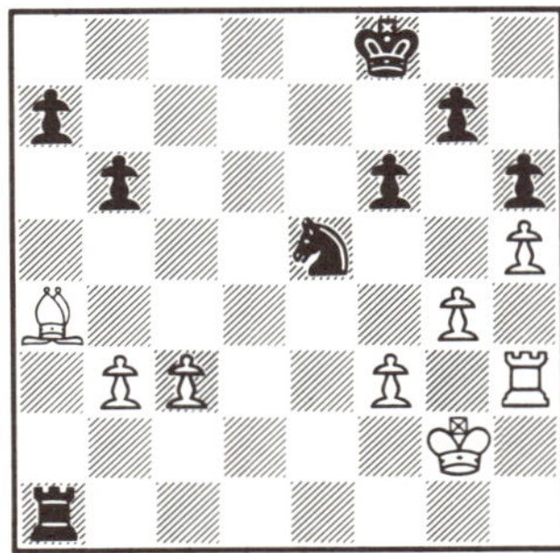

10. 1 ... Nd3. White sees the fork coming (do you?), and plays 2 Rh1. As so often happens with the N, if one plan is foiled he can quickly turn to another. 2 ... Ra2+ 3 Kg3 Nc5, forking White's B and P. Now White must lose a P.

11. When Black played 1 ... f6 to drive away White's B, he did not see White's clever reply. Can you see it? **[A3]**

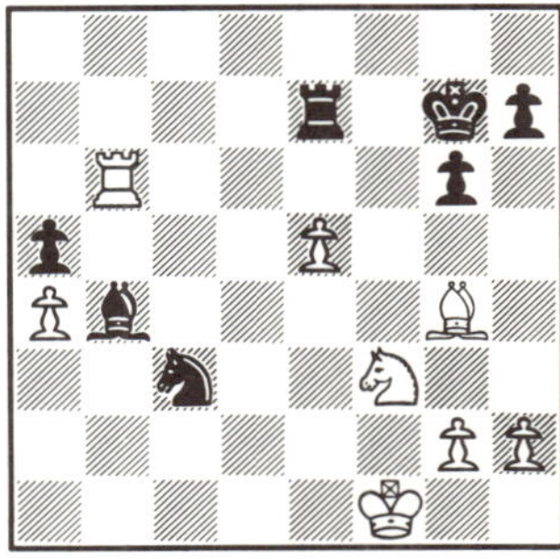

12. Black plays Nd5, forcing White to take a move to save his R. Black can then make the move he was planning all the time. Can you see what the move is? **[A4]**

Pins

1. *What is a PIN?*
When a man cannot move without exposing a more valuable piece to being captured, we call this a PIN. The man in the middle is "pinned" to his square because of the threat to the piece sheltering behind him. Diagram 1 shows an example.

Study Diagram 1 carefully, think about how a pin works, and then see if you can say why pawns and knights cannot pin an enemy man. All the other pieces can work pins.

2. *A pin can be serious*
A pin can be serious for three reasons:
* If the pinned man can be attacked a second time, it can sometimes be won for nothing.
* The pinned man can no longer support another man.
* The pinned man can no longer guard a square that may be vital. Diagrams 2, 3, and 4 show how pins can do these things. Study them carefully, for they have important things to teach you.

3. *Undo the pin when you can*
Since a pin can be annoying and sometimes dangerous, it is usually best to get out of it as soon as you can do so safely. You must remember that a pin that is doing no harm for the moment may become serious a few moves later. It is best to do something about a pin *before* it becomes serious.

There are three main ways of undoing a pin. They are:
* Moving the piece that is the target out of the line of fire (provided the pinned man is *still protected*).
* Placing another man of similar or less value *between* the pinned man and the target piece, provided *both* the pinned man and the man you have just moved *are protected*. This is called "breaking the pin".
* Removing the piece that is doing the pinning, either by capturing it or by forcing it to move away. Diagram 5 shows these three ways of undoing a pin.

Note there is another way of getting out of a pin. The pinned man can move quite safely if it

1. The white N cannot move because the black B would then capture the white Q. The white N is said to be "pinned against his Q". Is Black's N also pinned against his Q? **[A1]**

2. Black plays 1 … Be4+ 2 Ng2 If Black now plays 2 … h3, the white N is attacked a second time, cannot move, and must be captured next move. White must move his R. Why? **[A2]**

3. 1 f4 attacking the black N. If the N moves to safety, 2 R×g6! White saw that the h-pawn was pinned and was not defending the B at all.

4. Black's N and R on c8 are guarding e8, otherwise it would be mate. White plays 1 Bb2. Now things have changed! The N is no longer guarding the e8 square. How can Black avoid being mated? **[A3]**

5. White's N is pinned against his R. White can do one of three things: (1) move the R away; (2) bring the B back to e3; (3) drive the black B away with 1 a5. White also has a pin. Can you see it, and what can Black do? **[A4]**

6. The white B is pinned against the R and attacked twice, by the black R and N. But White has a lucky escape: 1 Bc4+, and when the black K moves, the white R can escape. Try not to leave your K on the same colour as an enemy B!

7. Each player has had a N pinned against his Q and each has broken the pin by interposing a B. If it is White to play, he can play 1 Ne5, and the black B on g4 is attacked three times and must either retreat or exchange itself for the white B on e2. If it is Black to move, there is an important difference. What is it? **[A5]**

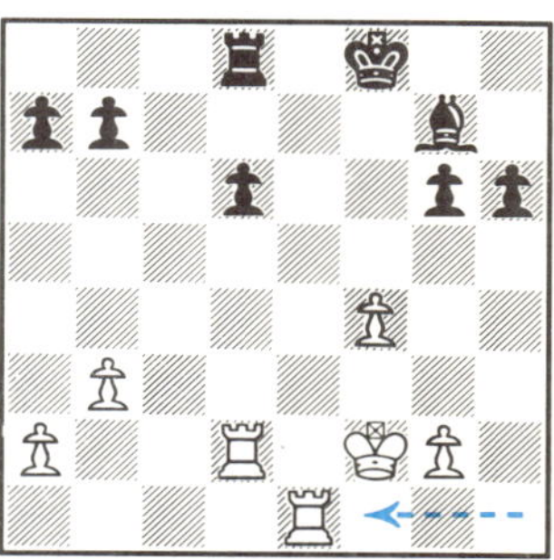

8. White's last move was a bad mistake. He overlooked the danger sign of two rooks on the same diagonal. He was planning Re6, forking two black pawns. But Black quickly took advantage of the danger sign. How? **[A6]**

can move *and* give check at the same time. See Diagram 6. Of course, if you have a man pinned in front of your *king*, that man can *never* move away, and the pin must be undone in one of the three ways explained above.

4. *When you have had a pin undone—look out!*

When a pin is undone, the piece that has been doing the pinning is sometimes in danger. So, if a pin of yours is undone, look out for your piece. Look at the white pieces in Diagram 7.

But sometimes the danger is even worse. Look at the black pieces in Diagram 7. In a case like this, you have to see the danger *before* it happens and take action first.

5. *Look out for the unexpected!*

If you have a strong pin on an enemy man and it cannot move, do *not* make the mistake of thinking this will last for ever. A few more moves can change things completely.

In particular, take care that your opponent doesn't arrange things so that he suddenly moves his pinned piece, allowing you to capture his "important" piece for nothing, because he has in fact started a deadly attack. Look back at the games given on pages 21 and 27. Play them over once again and see how one player makes the mistake of thinking a pinned piece will not move, and then, when it does, makes the further and fatal mistake of accepting the piece offered.

6. *Watch out for these danger signs!*

There are some danger signs that a pin may be coming. You must learn them so that you can take advantage of them and make sure your opponent cannot. The danger signs are:

* The queen and king on the same diagonal, file, or rank.
* A rook and king on the same diagonal, file or rank.
* The queen and a rook on the same diagonal, file or rank, especially if the queen is in front.
* Two rooks on the same diagonal. Diagram 8 shows an example. Now set up your board and try the other danger signs for yourself and see how they work.

Discovered attack

1. *What is a DISCOVERED ATTACK?*
When a man moves out of the way so that another piece can attack an enemy man, this is called a DISCOVERED ATTACK. The attack is *uncovered* when the first man moves and unmasks the fire-power of the second piece. Look back at Diagram 7 on page 35 for examples.

Any man can uncover an attack, but the attacking piece must be one of only three pieces. Which three? **[A1]**

Diagrams 1 and 2 give more examples of discovered attacks. Notice how unexpected a discovered attack can be (because it is disguised) and how it can upset the other player's plan completely.

You must be on the lookout for chances to use a discovered attack. Part of the secret is to time it so that it does the most damage. Diagram 3 shows an example of good timing.

2. *Discovered check*
If the attack which is unmasked is on the enemy king, it is *discovered check*! This is quite a powerful move because the player who makes it gets two moves for the price of one. It wins *a tempo* (compare page 26). Sometimes this can be deadly. Look carefully at Diagram 4, and make sure you don't get caught like that.

3. *Double attack*
Sometimes the man that moves to uncover the attack can *also* attack an enemy man. This is usually a strong move. If neither of the attacked men is defended, one of them is usually lost next move or the move after. Look at the white pieces in Diagram 5.

Sometimes the man that uncovers the attack also attacks the same enemy man as the discovered attack does. This, too, is strong. If the man that is twice attacked is undefended, it is lost, as it can now only be defended once. If it is defended once, the enemy must use a move to rush another man to its support. This again can "win a tempo" and give you a free move to advance to attack the enemy king. Look at the black pieces in Diagram 5.

4. *Double check*
Sometimes the enemy king can be checked twice at the same time, by means of a discovered

1. By moving his B, Black can uncover an attack on the white Q. White must take a move to save his Q and this means that the B's move is "free". For example, Black can play ... B×h3 then retreat his B next move having won a P and opened up White's K position. Or Black can play ... Bb5 and win the exchange next move (2 ... B×f1 3 R×f1).

2. Can you spot a discovered attack for White? 1 c5. Now Black must lose a P for nothing, and this could be very important so near the end of the game. N.B. If Black plays 1 ... a5, then 2 N×a5, and Black cannot play 2 ... R×c5 because of 3 N×b7.

3. Black's last move was g6. White sees that he has a possible discovered attack on Black's Q but that if he carries it out at once the Q has an escape square (e7). He also sees that Black is probably preparing to castle. So he opens the way for an attack on e7. 1 a4 Bg7 2 Bb5 attacking the Q and pinning the N. 2 ... Qe7 3 Ba3 and the Q is lost.

4. White thinks he has a mate on h7. He sees Black's discovered check 1 ... Ne4 dis ch 2 Kh1. If Black then plays 2 ... Nf6, he plays 3 R×f6!, with mate next move; or if Black plays 2 ... Ng5, he plans 3 h4, with mate two moves later. BUT – 1 ... Ne4 dis ch 2 Kh1 Ng3+! 3 h×g3 Qh5 mate!

attack. The strength of this move is that the enemy king *must* move (can you see why?) and this may expose it to fresh attacks. Look at Diagram 6.

5. *The discovered attack as feint*
In talking about forks (page 33) we saw how in chess you sometimes make a threat to take up your opponent's attention while you are really planning something else. One of the most important things about discovered attacks is that they often allow you to use this trick of pretending or "feinting". Study Diagram 7 and see how this works. If you have the possibility of a discovered attack, it is sometimes worth while asking yourself whether you can take a move or two to get things arranged so that you can use the discovered attack as a feint. Diagram 8 shows the sort of plan you can make.

This kind of attack is quite advanced chess for a young player, so do not be discouraged if you find it difficult to do in your own games. It will come with practice if you keep trying and refuse to be put off if you fail.

6. *Danger signs*
There are danger signs that can warn you that a discovered attack might be coming. These danger signs are:

* Your queen on the same file (or rank) as an enemy rook.
* One of your rooks (or both!) on the same diagonal as an enemy bishop.
* Your king on the same file, rank or diagonal as an enemy bishop, rook or queen.

If you see one of these danger signs, you should *at once* ask yourself if you can *safely* move your king, queen or rook out of the line of fire. If the answer is "yes", then do so without wasting time. Do remember this.

5. If it is White to move: 1 Be4. Now Black's Q is attacked by the white R and one of Black's rooks is attacked by the white B. Black must lose the exchange after saving his Q.
If it is Black to move: 1 ... Nh5. Now both the black N and Q are attacking White's R, which cannot move because it is pinned against the K. White must lose the exchange even if he defends his R.

6. Black to move: 1 ... Ne2 dbl ch (from the N and B). The white K cannot retreat into the corner because of the back-rank mate (2 ... Rd1) and so he must come into the open: 2 Kf1. Now 2 ... Nf4 threatening mate with ... Rd1. White must make a desperate exchange, 3 R×b6 a×b6.

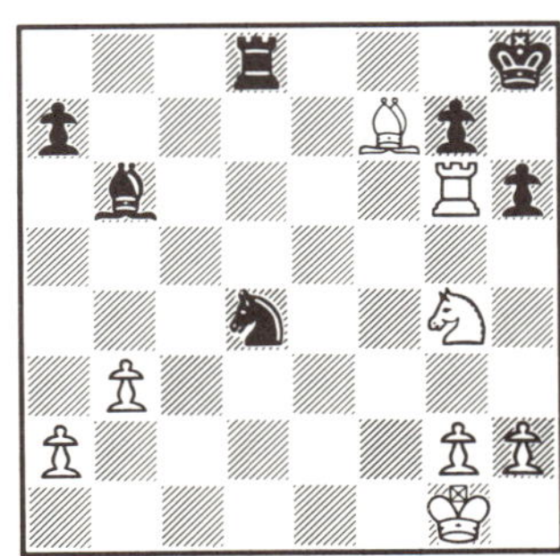

7. White has a really deep plan! 1 Ne4 Q×h4 (forced) 2 Nd6+ Kd8 (if 2 ... Kb8 then Q×b7 mate). 3 Nf5 dis ch Kc8 4 N×h4. White must now win, with his extra strength and good position.

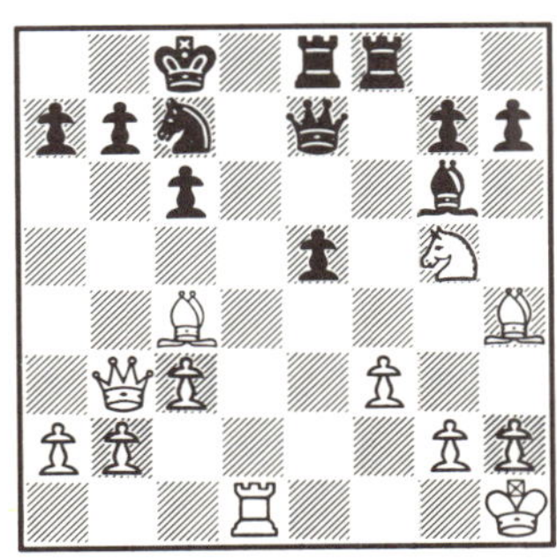

8. White sees a way of "engineering" a feint and a discovered attack. First he must get his Q on the right diagonal, and then get the black R to move: 1 Qb3 Bd7 2 Bb6 (a feint attack on the a-pawn) Qa8 3 Ng5! R×e1 4 Nf7+ Kg8 5 Nh6 dbl ch Kh8 6 Qg8 mate. Could Black have stopped the mate? **[A2]**

Exchange at the right time

1. *A fair exchange*
"Exchanging" in chess means capturing an enemy man in return for one of yours. Usually, you should make sure you get a *fair exchange*. If you read pages 10 and 11 again, you will see that a fair exchange should be a pawn for a pawn, a knight or bishop for a knight or bishop, a rook for a rook, or queen for queen.

But be CAREFUL! Sometimes such an exchange turns out to be not so fair after all. Diagram 1 gives a warning example. Take care not to be caught like this. Always work out the *effect* the exchange will have. Ask yourself two questions:

* Is my man protecting an important piece or square?
* What happens when I recapture?

2. *When to exchange*
Knowing the right time to exchange is one of the secrets of winning at chess and you will go on learning more about it all the time you play. But here are some helpful hints to start you off on the right road.

There are two main reasons for exchanging: to help you to attack and to help you to defend. We shall look at each kind in turn.

3. *Attacking exchanges*
The simplest example of an attacking exchange is when you force the exchange of an enemy piece that is guarding a key square. Diagram 2 shows what we mean.

An attacking exchange can also be used to open up lines for your other pieces. This is not so obvious, so do remember this use of exchanging. Look at Diagram 3 for an example.

Sometimes it is worth while making an exchange—even a poor one—in order to improve your development, that is to get your remaining pieces in better positions to attack. Occasionally this can bring immediate results. Study Diagram 4.

Sometimes you should even be prepared to "lose the exchange" to help your attack. (Look again at page 11 if you have forgotten what this means.) But be careful—if your attack fails, you will be worse off than before. Diagram 5 shows an example that meets with success.

4. *Defensive exchanges*
When you are under attack, you can often get out of trouble by exchanging off one or more of the attacking pieces for less active pieces of your own. Sometimes a defensive exchange like this is forced on you. When this happens, if your opponent is playing well, you will probably find yourself a little worse off after the exchange, even though you may have avoided the immediate danger. This means you have to take special care until you are quite sure the enemy attack has been beaten off. Look at Diagram 6 for an example.

Sometimes, however, when an enemy attack is under way, you can take the initiative and exchange off one (or more) of the most dangerous pieces when the attacker is not expecting it. If you do this successfully, you can not only destroy the enemy attack at a single blow but can sometimes move into a quick counter-attack. Study Diagram 7.

If you get into real trouble you may have to be prepared to "give up the exchange" (give up a rook for a bishop or knight). When this happens, it can be serious but not always fatal. If this destroys the enemy attack and the rest of your men are well placed you still have a fighting chance (Diagram 8). But if you have to give up your queen for a rook to avoid mate, you can expect to lose unless, of course, your opponent also makes a mistake.

A tip to remember
If you are a piece up (or a pawn or two pawns up in the end game), it is usually to your advantage to exchange off pieces to reach a winning end game.

5. *Beware of gifts*
If your opponent seems to be offering you his queen or a rook for a knight or bishop think twice before accepting, unless you are *sure* he has made a mistake. It could be a trap! Here is a game for you to play over and enjoy, which shows this in action.

	LASKER	A. N. OTHER
1	e4	e5
2	Nf3	Nc6
3	d4	e×d4
4	N×d4	Qh4
5	Nc3	Bb4
6	N×c6	Q×e4+
7	Be2	Q×c6
8	O–O	Nf6
9	Bf3	Qc4
10	Re1+	Kf8
11	a3	B×c3
12	b×c3	d6
13	Rb1	Bg4
14	R×b7	B×f3
15	Q×f3	d5
16	R×a7!	R×a7?
17	Q×f6!	Resigns

If 17 ... g×f6 18 Bh6+ Kg8 19 Re8 mate. If 17 ... Ra8 18 Qe7+ Kg8 19 Qe8+ R×e8 20 R×e8 mate.

1. Would 1 B×f6 g×f6 be a fair exchange for Black? Certainly not! See what follows: 2 Qg4+ Kh8 (or f8) 3 Qg7 mate.

2. The white N is guarding White's all-important h2 square. But Black can change that with an attacking exchange: 1 … B×f3 2 Q×f3 Q×h2+ 3 Kf1 Qh1+ 4 Ke2 R(f)e8+ 5 Kd2 R(b)d8+ 6 Kc1, and Black has a mating attack. Can you finish it for him? **[A1]**

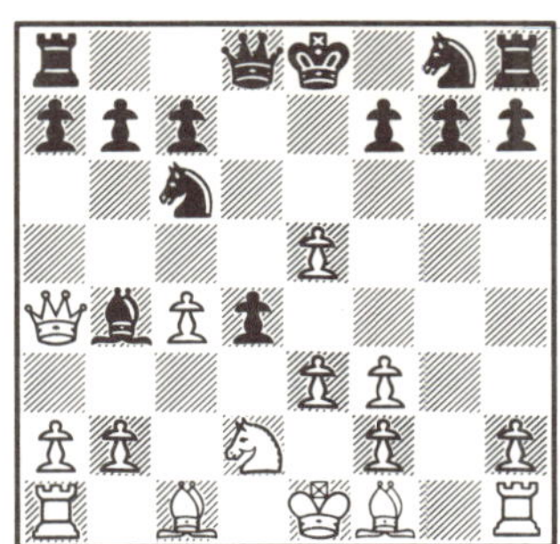

3. In this example, Black's simple P-exchange, 1 … d×e3 2 f×e3, opens up two lines of attack – the obvious d-file and the less obvious diagonal from h4 to e1. Black's next move was 2 … Qh4+, forcing the K to move and stopping White from castling. Note that if White had played e4 to avoid the exchange it would have left Black with a strong passed pawn.

4. White's dark-squared B is threatened, but instead of moving it away he decides to give up his N for two pawns. Not an equal exchange but here well worthwhile because of the grand position it gives White: 1 N×g5 f×g5 2 B×g5 threatening 3 Bf7+. Then if 3 … Kd7 4 Qg4 mate; and if 3 … Kf8 4 Be6 dis ch Ke8 5 Qh5+ Ng6, and Black loses his Q. In fact Black saw this and played 2 … Qd7; but White's better position won the game in 10 more moves. Try finishing the game for White. His next move is 3 Rf7.

5. Although he is two pawns down and his b-pawn is under attack, White played 1 Ne5! Black saw the *double* threat (2 Nf7+, forking K and R; *and* 2 N×c6, forking both rooks) and so he played 1 … R(d)c8. Poor Black! He had not seen a third threat: 2 R×f6! g×f6 3 Nf7 mate.

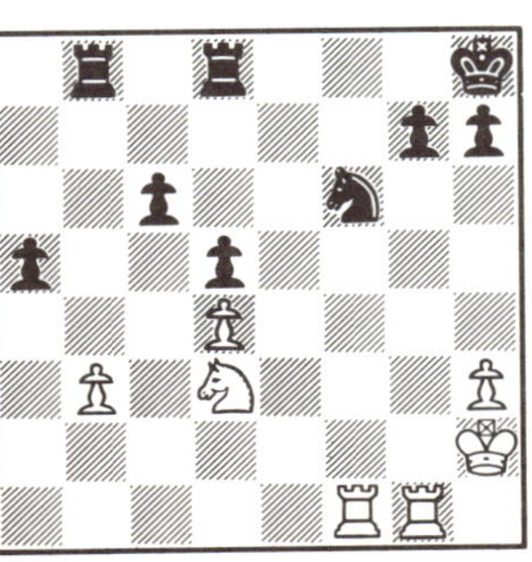

6. White's move, 1 e5, attacks a N and uncovers an attack on the unprotected B on b7. Black was forced to make a defensive exchange: 1 … B×g2. Instead of taking the black B in exchange, White played 2 e×f6 Bb7 3 f×g7 B×g7 4 Nf5 (thanks to the useful pin!), Bf8. Can you find White's next move, which made Black resign? **[A2]**

7. After 1 Bc3, White threatens mate with 2 Qg7. Black might be able to wriggle to safety by playing 1 … Kf7, but his best play is to destroy White's attack and then use his two extra pawns to counterattack. So: 1 … Qh4+ forcing White to exchange queens. Can you now win the game for Black?

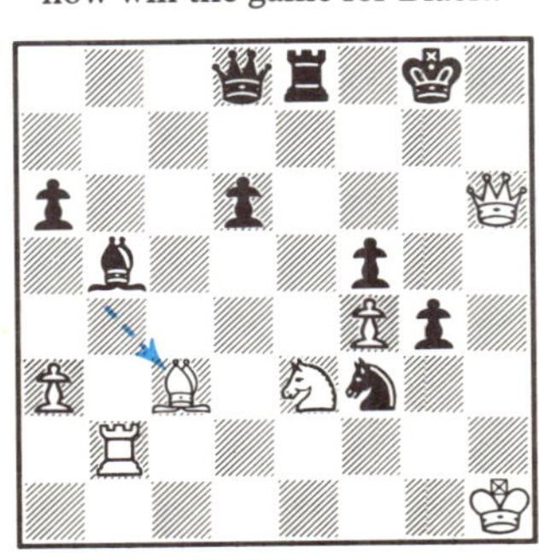

8. White played 1 Nf7+, expecting Black to reply 1 … Kg8. White then planned 2 Nh6 dbl ch Kh8 3 B×g7+ K×g7 4 Qg5+ Kh8 5 Nf7+ R×f7 6 B×f7, and Black cannot stop mate. BUT, Black decided instead to give up the exchange: 1 … R×f7 2 B×f7, and so won a tempo in which to play 2 … h6, to stop the fatal 3 Qg5.

Sacrifices

1. *What is a SACRIFICE?* When a player deliberately offers one of his men for nothing or in exchange for a less valuable man and his opponent accepts the offer, the first player has made a SACRIFICE.

Why should a player ever want to sacrifice one (or more) of his men? There are two main reasons:

* To get a mating attack
* To get a big improvement in position.

Sometimes one may be forced to make a sacrifice to avoid being mated (see page 39, for example), but here we are talking only of sacrifices that a player *wants* to make.

The young player usually finds that good sacrifices are difficult to see and plan—more difficult even than forks and pins. The following examples are meant to show you the kind of positions in which a successful sacrifice may be possible. Study the positions carefully and look for positions like them in your own games.

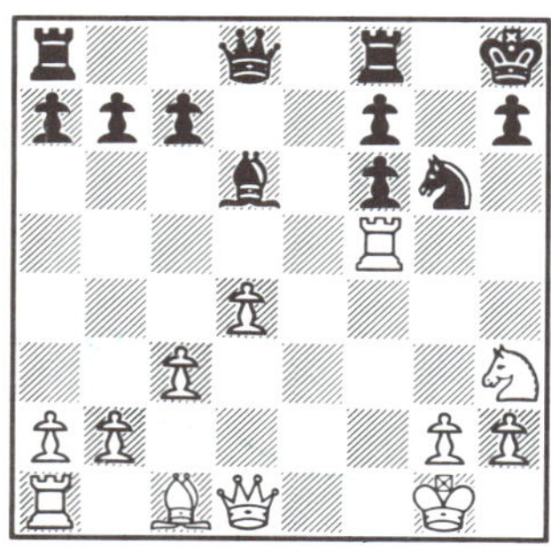

1. After White's 1 Qh5, Black was nervous and played 1 … Rg8. This freed f8 for his N, from where it could defend h7. Also his R could move to g7 to defend his h-pawn and f-pawn. But, alas, this defensive move gave White a brilliant sacrifice: 2 Q×h7+ K×h7 3 Rh5+ Kg7 4 Bh6+ Kh7 5 Bf8 mate.

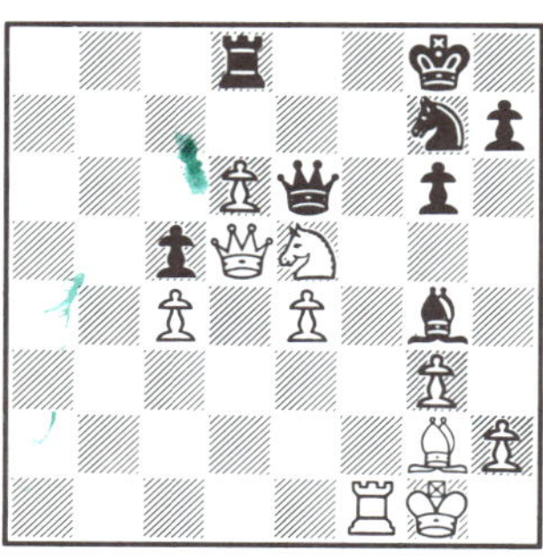

2. White has played Ne5, and Black seizes the chance to snatch White's dangerous d-pawn. 1 … R×d6. Now White calculates very carefully and plays 2 Nf7! Black thinks this is too good to miss: 2 … R×d5 3 Nh6+ forcing the K into the corner. 3 … Kh8 4 Rf8+ Qg8 5 R×g8 mate. Another back-rank mate!

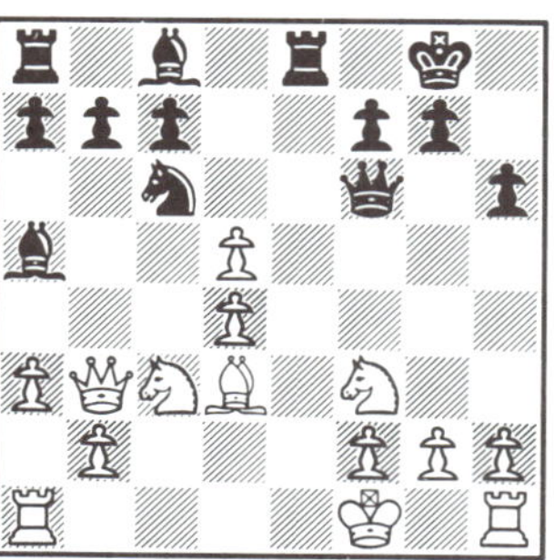

3. Should Black save his N and win back his P by 1 … N×d4? Black has a much better plan: 1 … Q×f3! 2 g×f3 Bh3+ (the reason for the sacrifice – to remove the g-pawn); 3 Kg1 N×d4 threatening mate with N×f3. So, 4 Qd1 defending the f-pawn. But now 4 … Re1+ forcing the Q away from the defence of the vital P. 5 Q×e1 N×f3 mate.

4. Although he is two pawns down, White decides to sacrifice more men to get into a winning position: 1 h×g3 N×g3 2 Qh2 N×h1 3 N×h4 Bg4 4 Bd3! B×d1. Black has captured two rooks and four pawns for one B and two pawns. But White now has a winning position. The game finished like this: 5 Nf5 Q×d3 6 c×d3 Bg4 7 Nh6+ g×h6 8 Q×h6 Nd7 9 Nd5 R(a)e8 10 Nf6+ Resigns.

2. *Sacrificing for mate.*
Usually this kind of sacrifice happens when the game has been going for some time, but just occasionally it can come quite early in the game. Look back yet again at the games on pages 21 and 27 and you will see two dazzling examples of sacrifices leading to mate early in the game.

A sacrifice can:

* Remove a man that is blocking your path
* Remove a man that guards a key square

Diagrams 1-3 show examples. *Note* that the squares just in front of the enemy king (usually f7, g7, h7) are favourite squares for sacrifices. So remember to keep a careful eye on your own f2, g2, and h2!

3. *Sacrificing for position*
Any sacrifice is worthwhile if you can be sure of mate. It is more difficult to be sure a sacrifice is worthwhile when it is made to improve your position. The difficulty is to know for certain when an improvement in position is worth giving up material for. Diagrams 4,5, and 6 should help by showing three examples in which the sacrifice is worthwhile. In each case the sacrifice leads to a strong attack.

Grandmasters can sacrifice in return for a *very* small improvement in position because they know how to use even such a small advantage to win. Ordinary players like ourselves are better not offering a sacrifice unless we can see either:

* a sure mate
* a clear, strong attack

4. *The gambit pawn*
There is one exception to what we have just said – quite often a player (almost *always* White) will offer to give up a pawn in the opening moves in order to get better and quicker development for his pieces. This is called "a gambit". Note that it's usually *not* a good idea to give up either of your centre pawns – they are too important. The usual gambit pawns are:

* c-pawn (the Queen's Gambit)
* f-pawn (the King's Gambit)
* b-pawn (the Evans Gambit).

In the Queen's Gambit and the King's Gambit the main reason is to lure one of Black's important centre pawns away from the centre. In addition, the King's Gambit offers a possible attack by the h-rook up the half-open f-file. The main reason behind the Evans Gambit is quick development of White's pieces.

5. *Sacrifices can backfire!*
Do be extra careful before offering a sacrifice. When it comes off, it is chess at its most exciting, but if you have made a mistake it can be serious. Look at Diagrams 7 and 8 for two awful warnings!

And here is yet another warning:

	White	*Black*
1	e4	e5
2	Nf3	Nc6
3	Bc4	Bc5
4	b4	B×b4
5	c3	Ba5
6	d4	e×d4
7	O–O	d×c3
8	Qb3	Qf6
9	e5	Qg6
10	N×c3	N(g)e7
11	Ba3	O–O
12	R(a)d1	R(f)e8
13	Ne4	Q×e4
14	B×f7+	Kf8
15	Bg8	d5
16	e×d6 *e.p.*	N×g8
17	Ng5	Qf5
18	Qf7+	Q×f7
19	N×h7 mate	

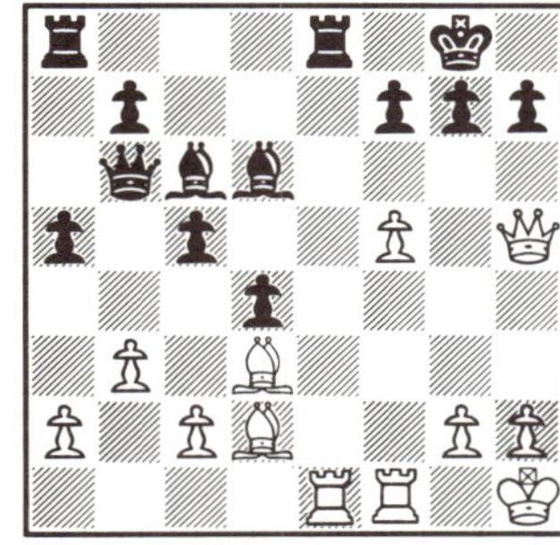
5. White believes he is strong enough on his K-side to crack open the black K position with a sacrifice. So, 1 Re6! If Black plays 1 … f×e6, then 2 f6 wins. How? **[A1]** Instead Black plays 1 … Qc7 2 Rg6. White offers his R again and this time Black accepts it. 2 … h×g6 3 f×g6 f6 4 Qh7+ Kf8 5 R×f7+. White offers his other R, but if Black takes it White mates in two moves. Can you see it? **[A2]**

6. White weakens his K position by moving his f-pawn and Black sees that he can get a strong position by a sacrifice: 1 … Qh4 2 g3 B×g3! 3 h×g3. Black now has a position he can build up into a winning attack. The game finished: 3 … Q×g3+ 4 Ng2 Bh3 5 Qe2 O–O 6 Qf2 Qg6 7 Be2 Rf6 8 f4 Nf5 9 Kh2 Qh6 10 Rh1 B×g2 dis ch 11 Resigns. (11 K×g2 Rg6+ 12 Kf1 Q×h1+, and mate next move.)

7. Black makes a good attempt at a winning sacrifice, but, alas, it doesn't quite come off: 1 … Rf3, threatening to win the Q for a R by Rh3+. White thinks his K-side pawns are good enough for a win and accepts the challenge: 2 g×f3 B×f3+ 3 Qg2 B×g2+ 4 K×g2 Bf8 5 h5 Kd8 6 h6, and Black must lose his two last pieces to stop a pawn from queening.

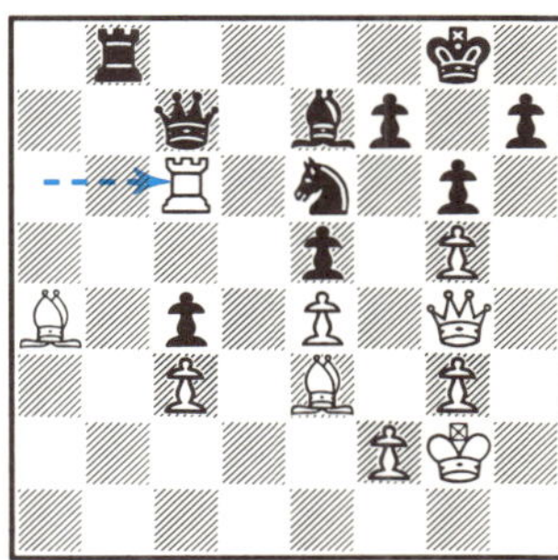
8. Black should get his Q to safety and double protect his N by 1 … Qd7. Instead he tries to tempt White into a sacrifice, with 1 … Qd8. White is very willing to be tempted: 2 R×e6, and Black plays his "surprise" move: 2 … Qc8, pinning the R and threatening f×e6 next move. But it was no surprise to White! 3 Bd7! Now if 3 … Q×d7, then 4 R×g6+ wins Black's Q. So White wins the black N for nothing.

Decoys and diversions

There are two very important questions that come up again and again in most games of chess. They are:

1. How can I make that enemy man move off that square on which he is stopping me doing what I want to do?

2. How can I open up paths for my long-range pieces to attack the enemy camp?

These questions are so important that we must study each of them in turn and learn how to answer them.

Making an enemy man move away
If you have read carefully so far and mastered what you have read, you will already know some of the ways in which you can make an enemy man move. To help you remember, here is a list of some of the ways you have met so far in this book.
* Attack the enemy man, for example with a protected pawn, or by a fork or discovered attack.
* Pin the man so that it cannot move.
* Exchange the man off for one of your own.

If you are in any doubt about how these ways work, read pages 32–39 again and, as you do so, think of how these tactics can be used to get rid of an enemy man that is hindering you.

Decoys and diversions
There are, however, other ways of making an enemy man move away. You can *tempt* him to move away by offering him a bait that he cannot resist or *divert* him away by making a fake (or feint) attack on another man. We call these tactics *decoys* and *diversions*.

You will remember that we have talked about sacrifices (pages 40–41). Please notice how a decoy move almost always uses a sacrifice as the bait that tempts the enemy man to move off the all-important square. Sometimes the decoyed man will be guarding an important enemy piece, sometimes it will be guarding an important square. Diagrams 1–3 show decoying tactics in action.

The decoy trap
Decoys can also be used to lure an enemy piece into a trap. Diagrams 4 and 5 show you what we mean.

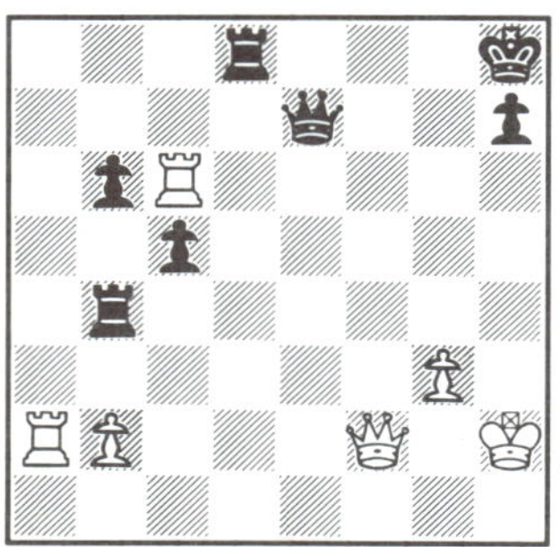

1. The black Q defends the R on the back rank. White sees that if the black Q could be lured away he could fork Black's K and R. So: 1 Ra7 Q×a7 . The Q is decoyed. 2 Qf6+ Kg8 3 Q×d8+, and mate follows in two more moves. How? **[A1]**

2. White seems to be in command. He is a P to the good and his pieces are threatening a K-side attack. But Black thinks up a decoy: 1 ... Rb7. White lets himself be diverted from his attack: 2 B×b7. But after 2 ... B×b7, suddenly it is the black pieces that look threatening (for example, 3 ... Q×h4 and 4 ... Qh1 mate).

3. Both queens have a pin against the enemy K. But White manages to decoy the black Q, with good results: 1 Nf7+ Q×f7 (forced – why? **[A2]**); 2 Bh5 (the decoy, pinning Q and R. If Black falls for the decoy with 2 ... Q×h5 then 3 Q×g7 is mate. If he sees the decoy and plays 2 ... Qf8, then 3 B×e8 wins the R for a N. Why can Black not capture the B? **[A3]**

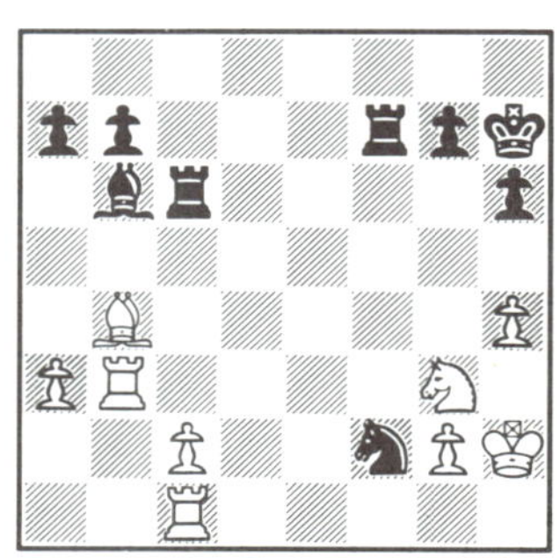

4. A decoy trap! 1 ... Be3, threatening a R. White didn't ask himself why he was being given a present: 2 R×e3? Ng4+, forking the R. Black wins the exchange. Remember this example – it is a very common trick to lure a piece on to a square on which it can be forked by a N.

Diversions

A military commander will sometimes send a small force to "create a diversion" on the left, while he makes his real attack on the right. Chess players often do exactly the same. They will, perhaps, attack a piece on the queen's side and when the enemy rushes reinforcements across to meet this threat, the real attack is launched on the king's side. Diagram 6 shows an example.

There is one more thing you should remember about using decoys and diversions. To be really worthwhile, the decoy or the diversion should bring some advantage *even if the enemy sees it and refuses to be taken in.* In other words the enemy has to choose between falling for the decoy and suffering a serious blow or refusing it and still suffering a less serious blow. Study Diagrams 7 and 8.

Have you noticed how decoys and diversions make use of forks, pins, discovered attacks, and sacrifices? This should help you to understand how terribly important these tactical tricks are and why you must learn to use them really well.

5. Black is a P up and his e-pawn looks as if it might queen. So, when Black pushed that P on with 1 … e4, White at once snapped it up: 2 Q×e4. BUT, 2 … Bd5, pinning the Q against the R. Black must win the exchange. Another successful decoy trap!

6. Black's Q supports his N on h6 and White wants to exchange that N off so that Black is forced to recapture with his g-pawn and open up his K position. He sees a diversion that will help: 1 a4 Na3 2 R×a3 Q×a3 3 B×h6 g×h6 4 Qg4+ Kf8 5 Qh5, with a strong attack even if Black avoids the immediate mate on f7.

7. White plays 1 Bc8, attacking a R. Can you see why? He has his eye on the f7 square! 1 … R×c8 2 R×f6 g×f6 3 Nf7 mate. If Black sees the trap and moves his R on a6 instead of taking the B, White wins a P with 2 B×b6 *and* still has a possible attack on the black K.

8. A refusal to be diverted! Black cannot play 1 … g×f6, because of 2 Q×h6+ Kg8 3 Rh5, with mate next move. So he tries a diversion instead: 1 … N×c3 hoping for 2 Q×c3 g×f6, but White pays no heed. 2 Rh5. Black tries again, with 2 … N×e2, but White presses on: 3 R×h6+ g×h6 4 Q×h6, mate. See that you play like White!

Opening and closing lines

Quite often, in order to get an attack going you have to open paths for your long-range pieces—your bishops, rooks, or queen. This means getting men *off* important files, ranks, or diagonals that you want to use. Remember that the men that need to be removed may be some of *your own men* as well as those of the enemy.

You should note that when chess players talk of an "open file", they mean a file with no *pawns* on it (even if there are one or more *pieces* on it). A "half-open file" is one with only one pawn on it. But when we speak of "opening lines" for attack we mean getting all men, pawns *and* pieces, off the line of squares you intend to use for your bishops, rooks, or queen.

Opening lines

A simple way to open a line is with a threat to the man that is

1. White wants to open a line of attack for his R on g1, so: 1 g4 f×g4 2 N×g4 and White threatens 3 Nh6+, with mate next move. If Black does not exchange pawns, White simply plays 2 g×f5 next move, and the line has been opened anyway.

2. Black sees that White's g-pawn is defended only by the white K. He can take advantage of this by opening up the long diagonal for his Q: 1 … Nc3. White must exchange because of the double threat (N×b1 and Ne2+, forking the Q). 2 N×c3 B×c3. Black's next move will be 3 … Bb7 and White will find it difficult to defend the g2 square.

3. Black sees that the white Q is undefended and on the same rank as his own. Can he use this fact, in spite of the 3 men in between the two queens? Yes, if he looks hard enough! 1 … N×e5 2 f×e5 (forced, or else 2 … Q×g3 is mate) Q×c4+, 3 Kf2 Be1+, and the white Q is exposed to her rival!

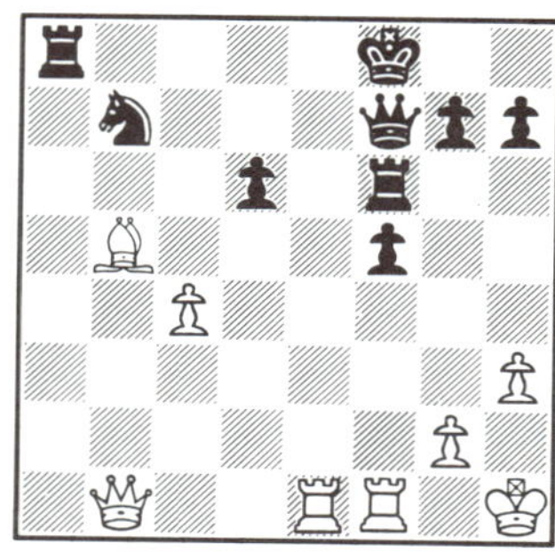

4. Black's f-pawn is defended by R and Q and looks safe and g6 next move would make it quite safe. But White sees a way to attack it by a diversion: 1 Bc6 Rb8 2 Bd5 Qc7 3 R×f5 R×f5 4 Q×f5+ with mate next move. Could Black have saved the game? **[A1]**

5. White's K is in check and he must close his g-file (otherwise … Qf3 is mate). So, 1 Bg3. The B is now pinned, so White must look out for an attack by the h-pawn. If Black plays 1 … h5, White must at once reply with 2 h4, then 3 Kh2 to unpin his B, and 4 Rg1, and White begins to muster his men for a counter-attack.

6. White's Q is badly placed and can hardly move. White sees that 1 … Bg4 would drive his Q to f2 and that this would allow Black to exchange queens. How can he stop this? Simply by closing the c8 to h3 diagonal by 1 f5. The P is well defended on f5 and the B on d2 now has a diagonal opened for it.

7. White has lost the exchange in return for a P and his a-pawn is under attack. Can he close the 3rd rank between his P and the enemy R? Yes, by decoying the black K on to a square on which it can be given a check. 1 N×g6 K×g6 2 Bf5+ Kg5 3 Bd3, and White has a breathing space to get himself organized.

8. Black has won material (B, N, and P for a R) but at the cost of having to face a nasty attack along the open f-file. He wisely decides to hand back a piece and close the file to the invading enemy: 1 … N(h)f6 2 e×f6 Kf7. The file is now closed by a blocked enemy pawn which White will have difficulty in shifting.

blocking it. Diagram 1 shows an example. But often it is not as easy as this. Then we have to think of exchanges, decoys, diversions, and sacrifices. An attacking exchange (look back at page 38) can sometimes open a line successfully, as in Diagram 2.

The last section showed how a decoy or diversion can lure a man away from his guard duty. They can be equally useful in opening lines for attack. Study Diagrams 3 and 4. You should particularly notice in all these examples how, before the line or lines have been opened, there seemed to be no attack possible. In each case one player has seen that if some men were out of the way things would be very different.

Always be on the lookout for attacks that would be possible if only a man or men could be moved aside. When you see such a possibility you can then plan how to get the men out of the way and the line opened.

Closing lines

Of course, when your opponent has open lines for his attack, you must set about *closing* them.

The simplest way of closing a line is by placing one of your own pawns or pieces on it so that it is blocked. Remember that the man you use to block a line must be well protected. The game may turn into a battle for that very piece, and you must be able to bring up extra men to support it, if necessary. Look at Diagram 5.

If it is not possible to block an enemy line with one of your own men, you must think of doing it by an exchange or even by a decoy sacrifice if the enemy is really dangerous. The exchange or sacrifice or decoy must be managed so that it ends with the line being blocked by one of your men or one of the enemy's in such a way that the blocking man cannot easily be dislodged.

It is worth noting and remembering that often a line can be most sucessfully closed by getting an enemy *pawn* on it, especially if that pawn can be blocked so that it cannot move forward.

Study Diagrams 6, 7, and 8 for examples of closing lines, using exchanges, decoys and sacrifices.

Here, for you to play over and enjoy is a game in which one player opens a line of attack early in the game and uses it to win decisively.

WESTMANN	WALTHER
1 e4	c6
2 d4	d5
3 Nc3	d×e4
4 N×e4	Nf6
5 N×f6+	g×f6

Black decides to open up the g-file and castle on the Q-side. From now on, the game revolves around the g-file, with White vainly trying to counterattack on the Q-side.

6 Nf3	Bg4
7 Be2	e6
8 O–O	

Perhaps White, too, should castle on the Q-side.

8 …	Bd6
9 c4	Rg8
10 Re1	Qc7
11 d5	Na6
12 Be3	O–O–O
13 Qa4	Bh3
14 Bf1	e×d5
15 c×d5	Rg4
16 Qc2	R(d)g8
17 d×c6	B×h2+
18 N×h2	R×g2+
19 B×g2	R×g2+
20 Kf1	R×f2 dbl ch
21 K×f2	Q×h2+
22 Kf3	Q×c2
23 R(a)c1	Qg2+
24 Resigns	

Mate next move cannot be stopped.

Keep your pawns strong

Many young players make the mistake of thinking that pawns are not really very important and that it doesn't matter *very* much if you lose one for nothing. YOU must not make this mistake.

In master chess, the loss of a pawn can often mean the difference between winning and losing. There are three reasons for this:

* pawns are valuable in defence and in blocking the movement of the enemy pieces (Diagram 1)
* they can be the spearhead of an attack, breaking through the enemy lines
* if you can queen a pawn that usually wins the game.

The rule is: KEEP YOUR PAWNS STRONG AND TRY TO MAKE THE ENEMY PAWNS WEAK.

1. *Strong pawns*

Pawns are strong:

* when they are *united*
* when they are *defended*
* when they are *free to advance*.

United pawns are pawns on ranks next to each other. United pawns are strong because they can support each other. This is true all through a game but can become especially important near the end of a game. Look at Diagram 2 for an example.

So the first thing to remember is: Keep as many of your pawns as you can united.

Defended pawns are strong because it is difficult for your opponent to capture them. The best

1. An excellent example of a pawn blockade. White has used his pawns very cleverly to hinder the enemy army. The black pieces are prisoners in their own camp, while White has the first three ranks open to his pieces *and* the valuable diagonal from b1 to h7 for his Q and light-squared B.

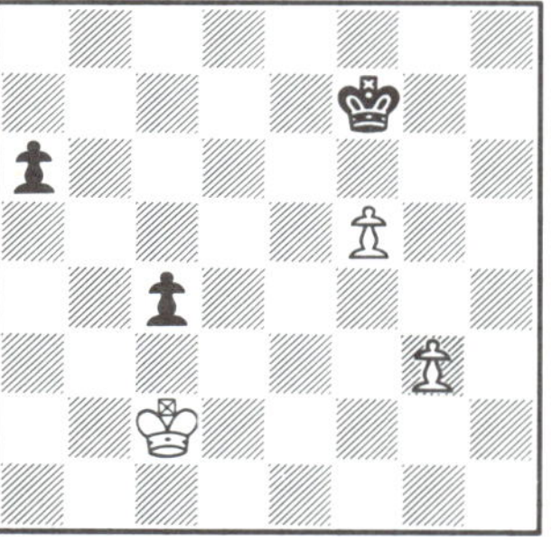

2. White's united pawns are very strong and will win the game. Black's isolated pawns are weak and cannot help him to win. It does not matter who has the move. Set up the board and try it yourself. **[A1]** If Black's pawns had been on the b- and c-files the game would have been a draw.

3. Look carefully at Diagrams (**A**) and (**B**). There is an important difference between them. In one postion the white pawn cannot be stopped, in the other it should not get through. Set up both positions and see for yourself which is which. Then try placing the white N in Diagram (**B**) on e4 and see if that makes a difference. **[A2]**

4. All the pawns are blocked. It is White to move. He sees a way of unblocking a pawn. Can you? 1 Nf5+. If 1 … Kh7, then 2 Kf6 wins Black's g-pawn and White's g-pawn is unblocked. If 1 … Kg6, then Ne7+ Kh6 3 N×c6 b×c6, and the b-pawn is free to queen. In the end game you must watch out for exchanges like that!

way to defend a pawn is with another pawn (united pawns!), but you will often need to defend a pawn with a piece or pieces, especially a key pawn that is under attack.

When this happens, there are two things to remember:

* a piece that is tied down to defending a pawn loses much of its usefulness
* a piece defending a valuable pawn should be placed where it cannot be attacked (e.g. by an enemy pawn) and forced to move, and where it cannot be exchanged off. Study Diagram 3. Defending pawns from behind by a rook on the back rank is often best.

Free pawns can advance, to attack, to control space, to reach a queening square. Sometimes this is possible simply because the way ahead is already clear. But you should take note that pawns that look blocked can often easily be freed, and these pawns are really as good as free pawns.

Study Diagram 4 carefully and make sure you can spot pawns that can be given their freedom. Such pawns should be carefully protected and freed and sent forward at the right time.

So, three things to remember: Keep your pawns united, defended, and free to advance.

2. *Weak pawns*

Pawns are weak:

* when they are *isolated* (not united)
* when they are *doubled* (two on the same file)
* when they are *undefended*, especially if they are also *blocked*.

Isolated pawns can be difficult to defend. Look back at Diagram 2. If you have to use your pieces to defend pawns you cannot use them to attack. This usually means that your opponent has the upper hand, since he is attacking and you are defending.

Doubled pawns are often weak, because they cannot both be defended by another pawn. Doubled, isolated pawns can be a real nuisance, as *both* of them can only be defended by using valuable pieces. Study Diagram 5.

If you have doubled pawns try to *undouble* them if possible. If your opponent has doubled pawns try not to let him undouble them.

Blocked pawns can become weak as they cannot move to get out of trouble. Weakest of all are pawns that are isolated, doubled, *and* blocked. Therefore; if your opponent has an isolated pawn or doubled pawns you should first block the pawn so that it cannot move and then attack it.

Sometimes a game can turn into a life-and-death struggle for a weak pawn, with the player that wins this struggle going on to win the game. Diagram 6 gives an example. Sometimes an attack on a weak pawn can be used to decoy the enemy forces away from the defence of their king. Once they are locked in battle over the pawn the attack is suddenly switched to the enemy king, often with quick results. Diagram 7 shows how a weak pawn can be used in this way.

3. *A game for you to enjoy*

Here to finish the section on strong pawns is an unusual game in which an advanced king's pawn decides things with dramatic suddenness.

1958-9 U S Championship

FISCHER	RESHEVSKY
1 e4	c5
2 Nf3	Nc6
3 d4	c×d4
4 N×d4	g6
5 Nc3	Bg7
6 Be3	Nf6
7 Bc4	O–O
8 Bb3	Na5??
9 e5!	Ne8?
10 B×f7+	K×f7
11 Ne6!	Resigns

Black must lose his Q or be mated. Can you see how? **[A3]**

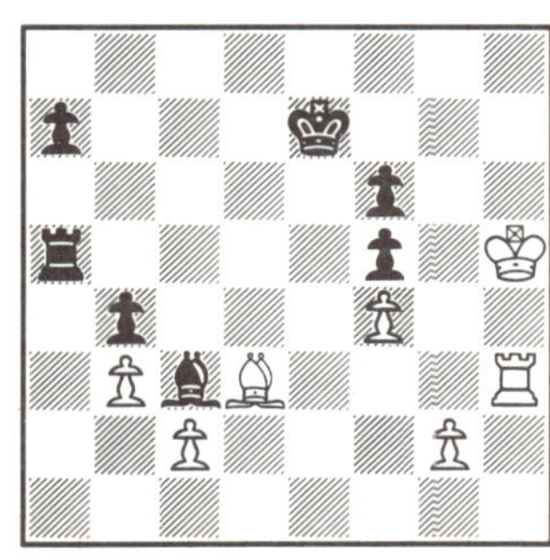

5. Black has a fatal weakness – that horror of horrors, pawns that are doubled, isolated, *and* blocked. He just cannot defend them. For example, 1 Kg6 Ke6 2 Rh5 and the P on f5 is lost. The P on f6 will soon follow. If Black tries to counter attack with 1 … Bd2, then 2 g3 Ke6 3 Bc4+ Ke7 4 Rh7+ and the P on f6 is lost.

6. It is important for White to hold on to his d-pawn, which seems well on the way to queening. So: 1 Rd2. Black, however, also sees that the white P is the key to the game: 1 … Ke6 dis ch 2 Kg3 Rd8 3 Nc4 b5 4 Ne3 R×d6. Or: 2 Ke3 (not 2 Ke4 because of 2 … Bf3+ and 3 … Bd5), Rd8 3 Nc4 b5 4 Nb2 R×d6.

7. White's extra, passed P is attacked and defended once. Black attacks it again: 1 … Nf6 2 R(f)d1 Qd7 3 Nc3 Bf4 4 Rc2 Bd6 5 R(c)d2. Now that the enemy forces are fully committed, Black suddenly switches his attack – 5 … R×f3! 6 g×f3 Qh3. White is in trouble; e.g. – 7 Ne4 B×h2+ 8 Kh1 Bf4 dis ch 9 Kg1 N×e4 10 f×e4 Q×b3. If 10 any other White move, then 10 … Qh2+ etc.

Queening a pawn

Pawns are important at every stage of the game. In the *opening*, they form a defensive barrier and, as they advance, they help to control the area near the enemy camp.

In the *middle* game, they are often the spearhead of an attack and sometimes one sacrifices itself to crack open the enemy defences.

In the *ending*, pawns can be very important indeed if there is a possibility of queening one of them. Of course, a pawn can sometimes reach the sixth or seventh rank in the middle of a game and, when this happens, it can be a very strong threat. Diagram 1 shows an example of this.

In this section we shall look at how to queen a pawn near the end of a game.

1. *Passed pawns*

A passed pawn is one that has no enemy pawns in front of it on its own file or on either of the nextdoor files. Diagram 2 shows passed pawns for White and Black.

The importance of passed pawns is this: *only passed pawns can become queens.* A passed pawn near the end of a game is very precious and MUST be protected. Of course, the ideal thing is to have two *united* passed pawns. This is very often strong enough to win the game, even against an enemy rook. Look back at Diagram 4 on page 10.

Often the best way to support a passed pawn is by a rook from behind. Diagram 3 shows what is meant. You should *never* get your rook (if you have only one) ahead of your pawn on the same file. It will have to come off the file to let the pawn queen, and when it does the pawn may be undefended and liable to be snapped up. Diagram 4 gives another example of how *not* to defend a passed pawn.

It is important to remember that a passed P can also win the game, not by actually queening, but by forcing the opponent to give up so much material to stop it that he loses anyway. In Diagram 3, for example, if Black gives up his R to capture the P, the white R and K will go on to checkmate him.

2. *Creating a passed pawn*

You must always be on the look-out for a chance to *create* a passed pawn. Sometimes this can be the main aim behind your plan, rather than a direct attack on the enemy king. Study Diagram 5 carefully to understand what we mean.

The situation in Diagram 6, or one like it, often occurs in games of chess. You must know how to create a passed pawn from such positions. Now try to make a passed pawn from the position in Diagram 7.

3. *The right sort of bishop*

The right sort of bishop to have when you are trying to queen a pawn is the bishop that can control the queening square. If you have this you can usually *either* queen the pawn *or* force your opponent to give up a piece to stop the pawn from queening.

Therefore, if you have a choice of pawns that you can push home to queen you should usually choose the one whose queening square is the same colour as your bishop. Study Diagram 8 carefully.

1. White has let Black's e-pawn penetrate his camp, thinking he can easily stop it queening. But sometimes an advanced pawn early in the game can bring things to a quick conclusion: 1 … Ng4! 2 f×g4 Qh4 3 g3 B×g3 4 h×g3 Q×g3+ 5 Bg2 Rf2, and White cannot stop the mate. Can you find a better first move for White? **[A1]**

2. White and Black each have a passed P, but White's is weak because its queening square is controlled by an enemy B. White's new Q will be captured immediately it is created, but Black's will live to win the game. Notice, by the way, how poor White's Q-side pawns are – doubled and isolated. They cannot get past Black's two pawns; the white K is too far away to help and the N is not as good as Black's B in this sort of end game.

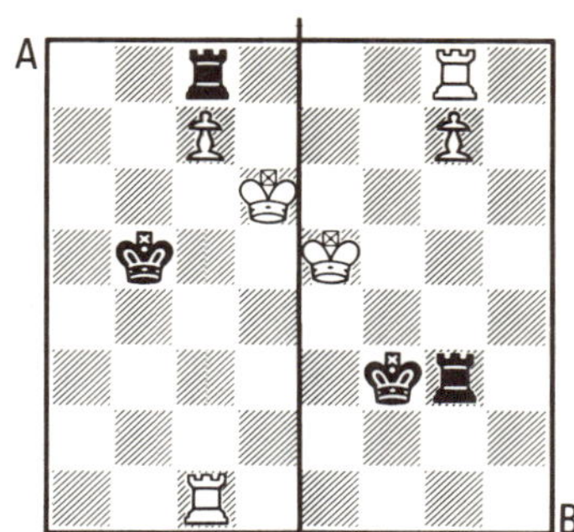

3. (**A**) White has a good passed P protected from behind by his R. As the white K has reached the P before the black K, White will be able to force the black R off the queening square. Black can stop the P only by giving up his R. (**B**) In order to queen his P, White must move his R off the queening file, thus leaving the P at the mercy of the black R. In this case however, White is lucky. He can check the black K, forcing Black to move it, and letting the P in to queen.

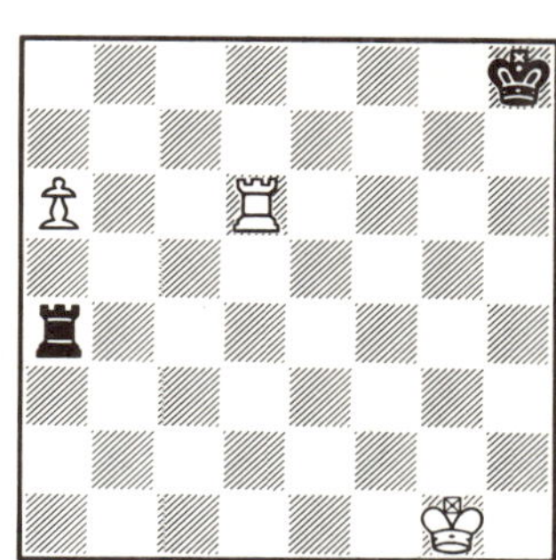

4. A passed pawn defended by a R from the side is weak, as it cannot advance without leaving the protection of its R. If an enemy R gets on the same file as the P, things are even worse. The only way the P in the diagram can queen is if its K can get to it before the enemy K and so help it home. Try it and see. Now put the white K on e5 and try again.

5. White knows that if he can unblock his c-pawn he should win. After a lot of thought he found quite a clever way: 1 Ne6+ Kg4 2 Nd4. Tricky for Black – if he leaves the B, then 3 N×b5 c×b5 and the white P is free. If he moves the B to safety, 3 N×c6, and again the white P is free. But Black doesn't give up: 2 … Bg1 3 N×c6 h5! 4 Ne7 B×g2 5 Nd5 (closing the diagonal so that the P can pass over c6) B×d5 6 K×d5 h4 7 c6 h3 8 c7 h2 9 c8 = Q+, and wins.

6. Creating a passed pawn. It is White to move. How can he be sure of getting a P through? 1 b6 c×b6 2 a6 b×a6 3 c6. White's P wins the race to queen. Note that plan only works if the enemy K is too far away to catch the P that has broken through. The rule is that the enemy K must be outside the "square" (shaded on the Diagram) when it is the pawn's turn to move. Try this "square rule" in other positions.

7. Can you queen a P for White? White must capture the black P, but clearly 1 Kc6 is no use because the black K would capture the c-pawn and the game would be drawn. So how does White do it? It is quite tricky, so here are the first moves: 1 Kb4 Ke4 – not 1 … Ke5 because of 2 Kc5 and Black is lost. Study the solution carefully as it has a lot to teach you. **[A2]**

8. In Diagram (**A**), White cannot win because his B is the wrong colour: 1 … Na4 2 b7+ Kb8, and the game is drawn. The black N will soon come round and win the P. In Diagram (**B**) the B is the right colour, and White wins: 1 … Nf4 (forking P and B); 2 g7+ Kg8 3 Bf7+ (forcing the K off the all-important square). The pawn queens and mate follows.

9 & 10. Here is a chance to put into practice what you have learned. In Diagrams 9 and 10 can you queen a P for White? White to move in each case. **[A3, A4]**

Use your King

The king can attack!
It is most important to remember that the king can be an aggressive, attacking piece. If it is being hunted, it can turn on its hunters and sometimes give them a nasty surprise. Diagram 1 gives an example. Don't forget that the king, too, can fork two pieces—look back at pages 32–3. Look also at page 23 and remind yourself that a king can separate a knight and pawn in the end game but not a bishop and pawn.

But above all, do remember to bring your king into action when there are few pieces left on the board. His help can make the difference between winning and losing.

The king can defend
The king can also play a vital part in defending his own position or one of his own men. Study Diagram 2. Sometimes the king can win a game by blocking an enemy passed pawn that would otherwise queen, leaving his own pawn free to advance. Diagram 3 shows what we mean.

The king as escort
Most important of all, however, is the part the king can play in escorting one of his pawns home to queen. When there are only kings and pawns left on the board, or king, pawns, and (let us say) a rook each, the king MUST march out to support his pawn.

The opposition
When the two kings are opposite each other, one square apart, and one of them has to move away next move, the *other* king is said to "have the opposition". Look at Diagram 4(A). If it is Black to move, *White* has the opposition. If it is White to move, *Black* has the opposition.

In end games with king and pawn against king, the opposition is very important. It is important because the enemy king *must* retreat or step aside and this should give you the advantage. If the player with the pawn can keep the opposition he usually wins. If the player without the pawn can keep the opposition, he can often draw the game.

NEVER forget the opposition in king and pawn endings. If you are trying to force through a pawn against a lone king, KEEP THE OPPOSITION and you should win. If you are defending against a king and pawn, KEEP THE OPPOSITION and you should get a draw. Here are some examples to show you what we mean.

King in front
If your king is in front of your pawn you must get the position shown in Diagram 4(B), that is, your pawn *two* squares behind your king. Then, if it is you to move, you can move your pawn instead of your king and so keep the opposition. Diagram 4(B) is a sure win for White if he plays correctly. Diagram 4(A), on the other hand, is a win for White only if it is Black to move (White has the opposition). It is a *draw* if it is White to move (Black has the opposition).

King at the side
If your king is at the side of your pawn it is an easy win if you keep the opposition until the enemy king is too far from your pawn to catch it. Study Diagram 5.

King behind
If your K is behind your pawn, it is most important to keep the opposition. Look at Diagram 6(A). It is a draw if Black does not let the white K get the opposition. Try it and see.

The weak rook's pawn
Of all the pawns, the two rook's pawns have the least chance of queening in a king and pawn ending. A rook's pawn can be forced through to queen only if you can stop the enemy king reaching the rook's file in front of your pawn. Diagram 6(B) shows you why. This is one of the few king and pawn endings in which the opposition does not matter.

Some good advice
* If you have to move your K across the path of one of your own men, make sure the man cannot be lost through a check. (Diagram 7.)
* When an enemy B is about, take care before placing your K and another man on the same diagonal of the bishop's colour.
* When an enemy N is about, look out for forks.
* Beware the unexpected sacrifice or exchange.
* Make sure your king is not shut out from the field of battle.
* Beware perpetual check. (Diagram 8.)

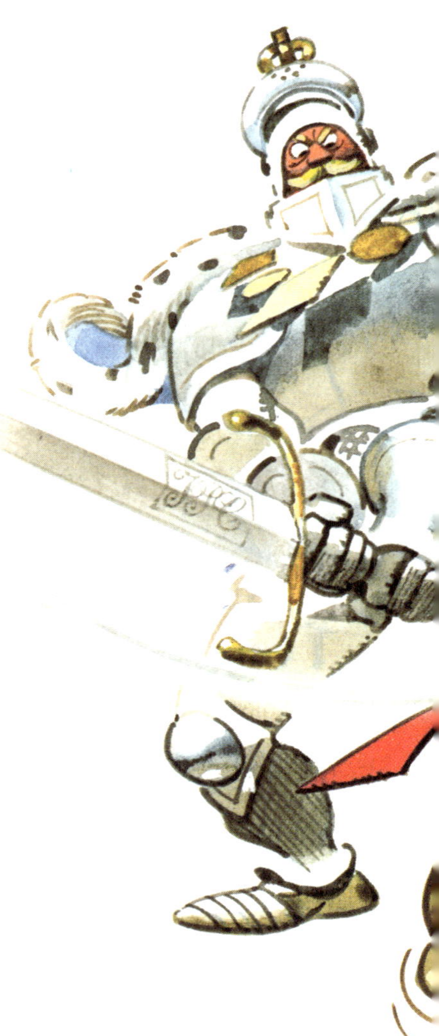

1. White thinks he can drive the exposed black K towards his own K and N and into a mating net: 1 Qe8+ Kf6 2 Qf8+. Black thought carefully and decided he could use his K if White went on checking with his Q. So: 2 … Ke5 3 Qe7+ Kf4 4 Qd6+ Ke3 5 Qe5+ Kf2. Suddenly White has no more checks and the black K captures the g-pawn next move, with the threat of … Q×f3 to follow. Black's K march has improved his position.

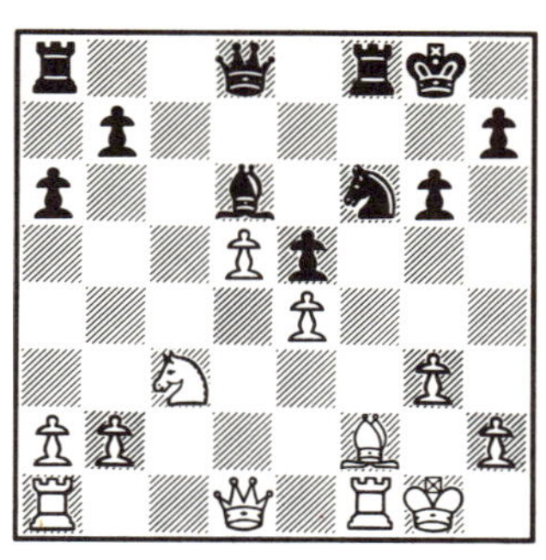

2. White plays 1 Qb3 and Black defends the b-pawn with 1 … Qc8. But White is on the alert and sees that this is an attacking move as well as a defending one. Can you see what Black is planning? White foresees 2 … Qh3 and 3 … Ng4, and he is in trouble; for example – 2 R(a)c1 Qh3 3 Kh1 Ng4 4 Bg1 (to stop the mate) R×f1 5 R×f1 Q×f1 and White has lost a R. What can he do to stop this? **[A1]**

3. Black has an important decision to make. By counting the moves, he calculates that if White captures the g-pawn, the a-pawn will have time to queen. So he works out what happens if White sees this too: 1 … a5 2 Kf5 a4 3 e6 a3 4 e7 a2 5 e8=Q a1=Q. This is not good enough for Black. Can you work out what happens if he uses his K to block the e-pawn? **[A2]**

4. The importance of the opposition. Diagram (**A**) will be a win for White only if it is Black to move. If it is White to move, the game will be drawn. Diagram (**B**) is a win for White no matter who has the move. The text explains why. Now set up each position in turn and try for yourself. Possible moves are given in the Answers. If you are in any doubt study them very carefully. **[A3]**

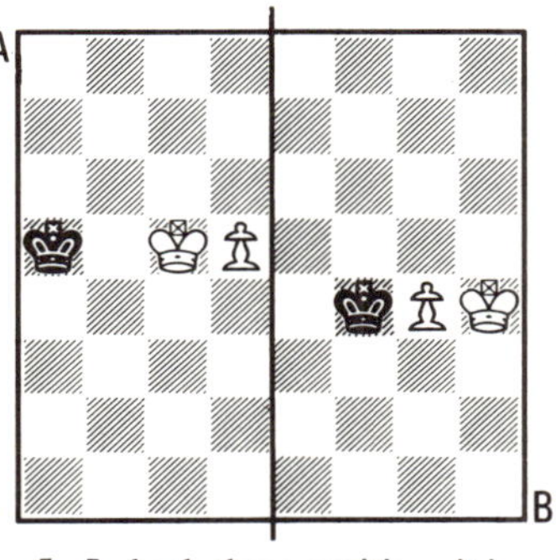

5. In both these positions it is an easy win for White no matter who moves first. In Diagram (**A**) if the black K moves up the board, the white K must move up, too, to keep the opposition until it is safe to move the P forward. If White has the move, he moves the P to keep the opposition. In Diagram (**B**), the white K *must* keep the opposition to stop the black K moving in front of the P.

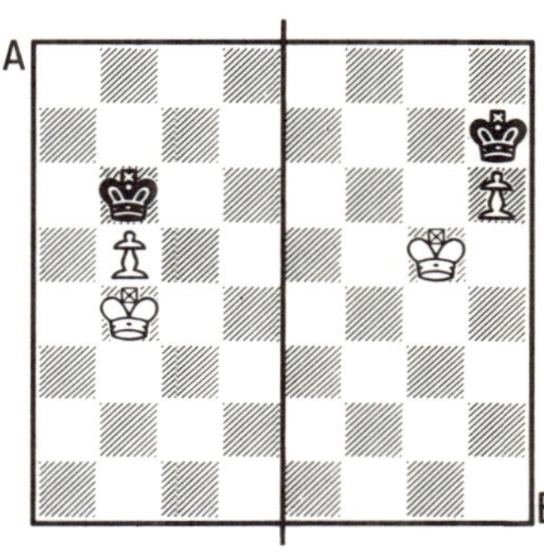

6. In Diagram (**A**), it should be a draw no matter who is to move, because Black can keep the opposition. The secret is for Black to move straight back until he can take the opposition whenever he can. If White is allowed to get the opposition he can win. In Diagram (**B**), White cannot force the black K out of the corner and the game is drawn. Try both positions for yourself. **[A4]**

7. 1 Rg2+ Kf7 2 Kg5 (to capture the h-pawn) Rg8+ and wins a R for a P.

8. 1 Qc2+ Kh8 2 Qc6 Qe5+ 3 Kg1 Qe1+, and White can only avoid perpetual check by giving up his b-pawn.

Plan... plan... plan...

Always have a reason!

EVERY move you make in a game of chess should have a reason. Usually a move does one of three things. It should help you to:

* attack * defend * develop.

Quite often a move does two of these at the same time, and occasionally a single move can do all three at once! Can you find a good move for Black in Diagram 1?

Before every move you make you should ask yourself why you are making the move. If you cannot say why, if you cannot see how the move will help you to attack or defend or to develop, DO NOT MAKE THAT MOVE. Take a little longer to think and find a better move.

Always have a plan!

Having a reason for a move is not the same as having a *plan*. A reason may last only for a single move, and the reason for the next move may be quite different. A plan lasts for several moves—in fact it could last till the end of the game, especially if it is a winning plan. A plan is a *long-term reason* for the moves you make. Diagram 2 shows an example of long-term thinking.

Of course, every player wants to *attack* and will try to make an *attacking plan*. But, if your opponent has got the better of the opening moves, you may find that you have to make a *defensive plan*, before you can think of attacking. In any case, you should make sure your defence is sound before you think of attacking.

The first step in making a plan of any kind is to look for *weaknesses* in your own position and in the enemy position. You should then set about defending your own weak points and afterwards attack the enemy weak points.

Defend your weak points

Here are some of the weak points you must defend:

* Weak squares or weak pawns
* "Holes"
* Dark- or light-squared weakness
* Open files or diagonals.

1. The centre of the board has been cleared by exchanges, and White now thinks of getting ready to attack. He sees two possible squares for his N: c4 and e4. On either square, the N would be protected by a P and either move would make a double attack on Black's B which is defended only once. The N would be better placed on e4 for an attack on Black's K, so White decides on 1 Ne4. What would you reply for Black? **[A1]**

2. Black is a pawn up and is threatening to capture another one with ... Q×a3. White can easily defend the a-pawn with 1 Ra1 and could perhaps trap the black Q with 2 R(f)b1. On the other hand, Black will probably see the trap and get his Q to safety by 1 ... Qb6 and 2 ... Qc7 defending the b-pawn, and White is not much better off with both of his rooks off centre. White wonders if he can use his forward f-pawn to make a counterattack. Can you work out a plan for him? **[A2]**

3. Black looks at his own position and White's position before making his plan. This is what he thinks: "My K is not very well defended and I must be careful of the long open diagonal controlled by White's B. My e5 square is rather weak. I can close the diagonal by playing ... Nd4. If White's N were away I could mate him with Q×g2 mate and, if I move my N, my B is also threatening that same weak square and h1. Can White defend with these weaknesses? If he plays Rf2 defending g2, what should I do?" **[A3]**

Weak squares and weak pawns
Squares or pawns can become weak if they cannot be easily defended, especially when they cannot be defended by a pawn. "Backward" pawns are often weak as the pawns next to them have advanced, leaving them behind. Doubled pawns are often weak, especially if the front one is blocked. Squares near your back rank, especially squares near your king can be very serious weaknesses. Look at Diagram 3.

If you have weak squares or pawns to defend, remember what you have learned about closing lines (pages 44–5) and defensive exchanges (pages 38–9). Remember also how to keep your pawns strong (pages 46–7).

Holes
A "hole" in a chess position is a square in front of a pawn that cannot be defended by neighbouring pawns. Look at Diagram 4. If you have allowed a dangerous hole to develop, your plan must include preventing the enemy from settling there, as White and Black have to do in the diagram.

If you can occupy a hole in the enemy camp you do two things: (1) You get a stronghold inside the enemy lines and often control important squares near his king. (2) You block the backward pawn, and if this is still on its starting square (as in both of Black's holes in the diagram) it can cramp the enemy's movements very severely. Black's holes are on c6 and g6. The first is far enough away from his king not to worry him; but the other is far more serious. An enemy piece on g6 would put his king in great danger. It is difficult to defend the hole as it is controlled by a white P.

Weakness on dark or light squares
This can be a difficult weakness to spot. If you look again at Diagram 4 you will see that Black is weak on the light squares, especially the light squares near his king. He has no light-squared bishop to defend them, and *all* his pawns are on dark squares. A pawn on a dark square controls only dark squares. This is another weakness that Black's defensive plan will have to put right. Diagram 5 shows another example.

Open files and diagonals
You have already learned about the importance of open lines (pages 44–5). Read those pages again and always remember the importance of open files and diagonals when you are making your plan for defence or attack.

Destroy enemy strongpoints
If the enemy has a strongpoint too near your camp for comfort, you should usually plan to destroy it before planning your own attack. Look at Diagram 6 for an example of what is meant.

Of course, it is best not to let the enemy build strongpoints, but any that he does construct should be destroyed or neutralized.

Attack or occupy enemy weak spots
When you find weak spots in the enemy camp, you should plan to attack them. All the diagrams in this section give you examples of this in action. Make sure you understand what the player's plan was and what the reason was for every move that was considered and why some possible moves had to be rejected.

Planning practice
To end this section, Diagram 7 gives you some practice in planning.

4. White and Black both have holes in their positions. White has a hole on b4 (occupied by a black B) and another on d4. The black B is a nuisance because it hampers both of White's rooks, so White decides he must exchange it off. How can he do this? It would also be a nuisance if the hole on d4 were occupied by Black's B (another reason for getting rid of it) or by Black's N, which could control squares uncomfortably near White's K. How can White stop this? **[A4]**

5. Here is a list of strengths and weaknesses in White's position. *Strengths* 1. Every man is protected. 2. Lines are open for attack or defence. 3. Rooks are united, centrally placed, and one controls the only open file. 4. His two bishops could be valuable in an end game. *Weaknesses.* 1. The d-pawn is isolated. 2. The d5 square is weak and if occupied by a N could hamper White's bishops. 3. A hole on g3. Now make a list like this for Black and then make a plan for White. **[A5]**

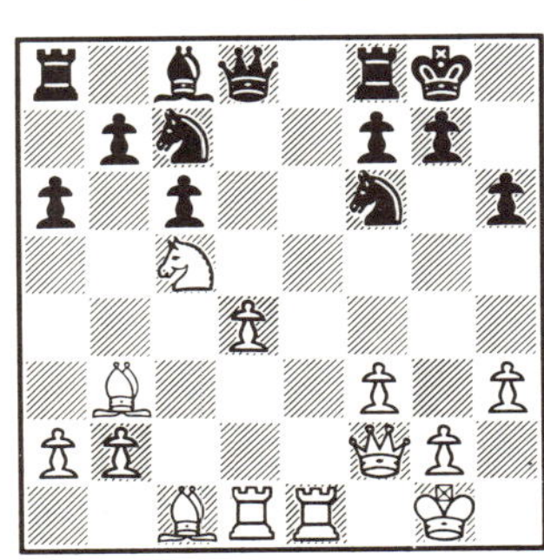

6. Material here is equal, but Black looks in a much stronger position. He has got his B settled in the hole on g3, where it protects and is protected by the f-pawn. From there it hampers the movement of White's R and K. How can White get rid of the troublesome B? Obviously, sacrificing the exchange by 1 R×g3, f×g3 is not good for White. The only piece of equal value he can exchange for the B is his N. How can he force the exchange? **[A6]**

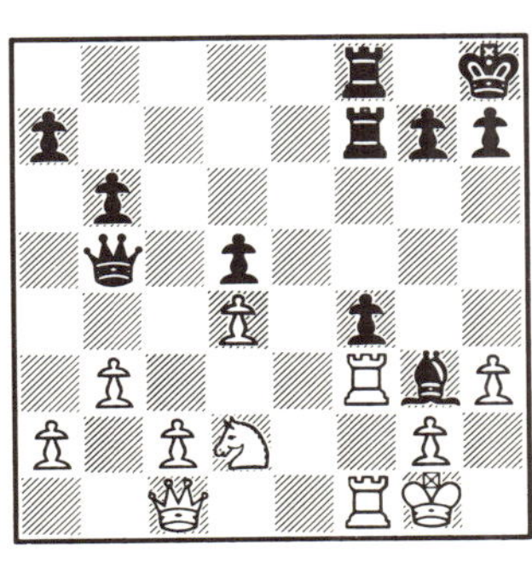

7. Here is a position from a game. The opening moves were: 1 e4 e5 2 Nf3 Nc6 3 Bb5 Nd4 4 Bc4 Bc5 5 N×e5. White could not resist snapping up the free P, and making a double attack on the f-pawn. Black could have parried that by 5 ... Ne6. Instead he played 5 ... Qg5! What replies by White did Black have to consider before making his fifth move and what did he plan to do in each case? **[A7]**

1. White's first task is defensive – to stop Black from queening the h-pawn. But can you find a plan for White that will do this *and* allow him to move into the attack? **[A1]**

2. White looks to be in all sorts of trouble – 1 ... Nh3+ wins his Q, for a start; and the f-pawn is very threatening. Is there a plan for White that will save the game? **[A2]**

3. Material is level and though White's Q and N are both attacked, he can easily use the Q to defend his N. But suddenly he saw a way of winning material. Find his plan. **[A3]**

4. Black is mated in 4 moves if White plays 1 g4! (How?) But White chose to play 1 Qh8+ first, and Black was able to wriggle out of the mating net. (How?) **[A4]**

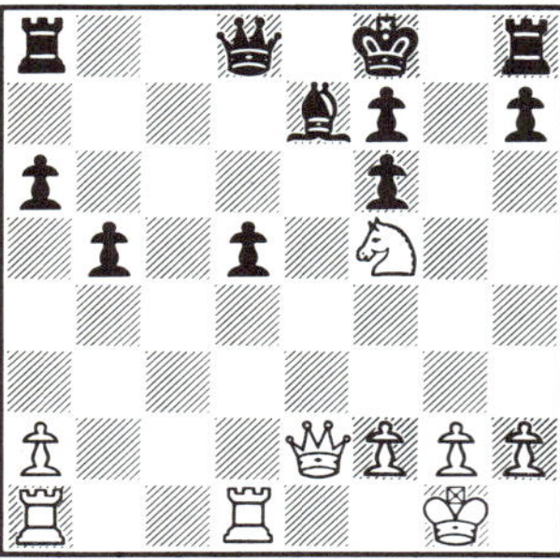

5. Black plays 1 ... h5 to stop 2 Qh5 and then Qh6+. White, however, had another plan ready which was even better. What was it? *Hint*: think decoys. (Spassky (12 yrs of age) *v* Avtonomov, Leningrad, 1949.) **[A5]**

6. White's B is pinned against his Q and is attacked by the h-pawn. White could defend it by 1 Rh3 (if 1 ... h×g5, then 2 Qh8 mate). But White found a better plan. *Hint*: remember the warning on page 35! (Torre *v* Lasker, Moscow, 1925.) **[A6]**

7. Black is in a strong position, but must look out for 1 R×e4 followed by Re8 mate. He plans to capture White's N. Can you see how he did it? (Botvinnik *v* Bronstein, World Championship, 1951 Game 11.) **[A7]**

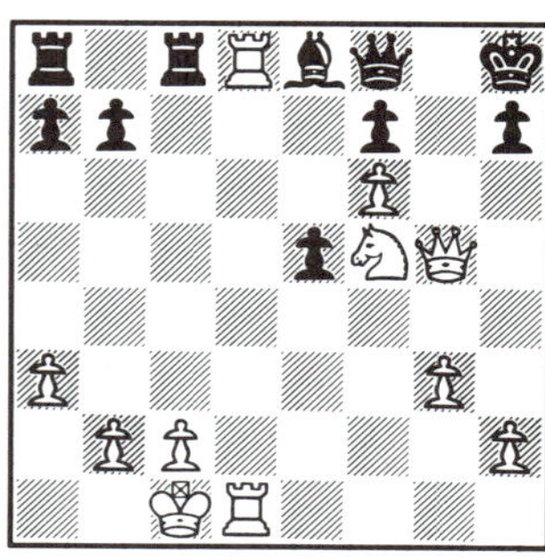

8. White must do something about his R on d8. To exchange rooks would help Black and to retreat his R would spoil his attack. White thought up a plan involving a N fork. Can you see it? (Em. Lasker *v* Réti, New York, 1924.) **[A8]**

9. White has sacrificed a B for his attack, but how does he plan to continue? Can you find the four brilliant moves that forced Black to resign? (Gligoric *v* Petroshan, Belgrade, 1954.) **[A9]**

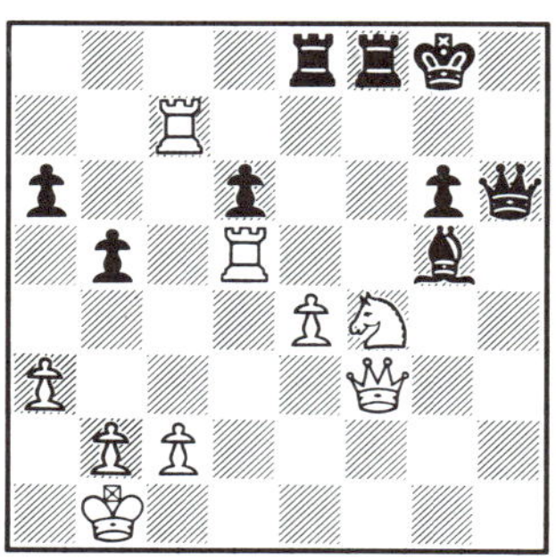

10. White has lured Black into attacking the white N and then prepares a devastating blow: 1 Qb3. Black obliges: 1 ... R×f4. Why did Black resign after two more moves? (Fischer *v* Bolbochan, Stockholm, 1962.) **[A10]**

11. White's plan here was to lure Black's major pieces away from the defence of his K by offering Black a chance of a mating attack! So: 1 Rd3 Rb2 2 Bg1 Qa1 3 Bf2 Rb1. Black planned 4 ... Rh1 5 ... Qf1 6 ... Qh3 mate. But what was White's plan? (Lasker *v* Showalter, Cambridge Springs, 1904.) **[A11]**

12. Here is a chance to practise analysing variations. White's N is attacked and after much careful thought White played 1 Ng5. Before moving he considered six possible replies by Black. List the six black moves and work out what White planned to do in each case. **[A12]**

Planning an attack

Before you attack
There are some things you must make sure of *before* you launch an attack. It will help to ask yourself three questions:

* Is my king safe? No threat of a back-rank mate?
* Are all my men safe?
* Can I bring my pieces back quickly if I suddenly need to defend my king?

You must be able to answer "Yes" to these questions before it is safe to attack.

When you attack
If you have spotted a weakness in the enemy position, you have a target to attack.

* Is there a weak square I can build into a strongpoint?
* Is there a weak pawn I can attack and win?
* Can I make a direct attack on the enemy king?

If you answer "Yes" to one or more of these questions, you have an obvious target to attack. But sometimes the enemy has no obvious weakness and then you must ask yourself: Can I break through the enemy defences:

* in the centre?
* on the queen's side?
* on the king's side?
* by a pawn advance?
* with my pieces?
* by a sacrifice?

One important decision you have to make in planning your attack is:

* Do I attack the enemy king?
* Do I attack to push a pawn through to queen?

Sometimes these two can be combined, but usually you should have a clear idea *which* you are trying to do.

Two more things before we end with some planning practice.

After you have made a plan, be prepared to change it if you have to. Your opponent may find a good move that you did not expect. Perhaps he may make a mistake that gives you an even better opportunity. In either of these cases, you must be ready to change your plan. Don't stick to a plan at all costs.

Lastly, remember that even a poor plan is better than no plan at all. If your plan fails, you will have learned something. The sure way to improve your chess and win more games is to make a plan *every* time. Gradually your plans will get better and as your plans get better, so will your chess.

To finish, here are some positions to test what you have learned about planning and to give you practice in making the kind of decisions you will have to make in your games.

Notation

Before you can get very far with learning about chess from a book, you must learn to *read* chess games.

Chess games are written in a kind of shorthand which we call NOTATION. In other words, they are "noted" down on paper in a kind of code. Chess players must be able to write down their own games as well as read other people's games. It is only because of this use of notation that we can still play over on our own board famous games from the past and learn from them.

There is more than one form of Notation, but the one we shall explain is called Algebraic Notation. This system is used in all official chess competitions to record the games played. The three important things to know are:

1. The *man* that is being moved
2. The *file* to which the man is being moved
3. The *rank number* of the square to which it is being moved.

The names of the men are shortened to a single letter:

Pawn = P

Knight = N

Bishop = B

Rook = R

Queen = Q

King = K

The *files* are named a,b,c,d,e, f,g,h, from left to right, as White looks at the board.

The *ranks* are numbered 1 to 8 *from White's side* of the board. See diagram 1.

The name of each square is made up of its file code and its rank number. For example White's King begins the game on e1 and Black's King on e8. Each square has only one code name, which is the same for both White and Black moves.

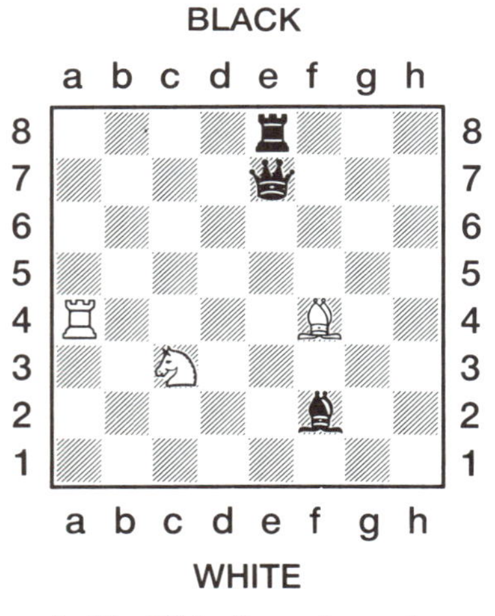

1. The White R stands on a4 and the Black B on f2. Now name the squares the other pieces stand on. **[A1]**

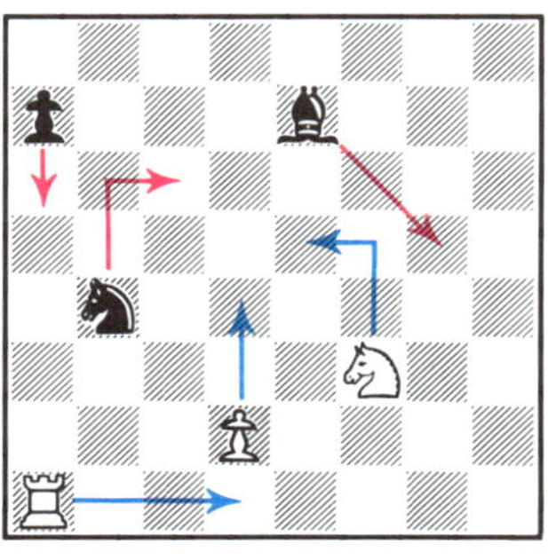

2. Name the squares each man stands on and then write down the moves shown by the arrows. **[A2]**

Other signs you need to know are:

× = captures

+ = check

++ = checkmate

O–O = castles King's side

O–O–O = castles Queen's side

e.p. = en passant

dis ch = discovered check

dbl ch = double check

! = good move

? = poor move

e8=Q (or N) = pawn queens (or becomes a N)

Moves are written down like this:

Bg5 = Bishop moves to square g5

Qb8 = Queen moves to square b8

N×c4 = Knight captures the man on square c4

R×c1+ = Rook captures the man on square c1 and gives check

A point to note is that when the man being moved is a pawn it is usual to *omit* the sign P. If White begins by moving his King's Pawn two squares forward and Black does the same in reply, the moves would be written: 1 e4 e5.

When the pawn move is a capture, the pawn making the capture is given the name of the file it stood on before moving, like this: c×d4 (= the pawn on the c-file captures the man on d4).

When both Knights or both Rooks could make the move the correct piece is shown by naming the file it stood on before it moved, like this: N(d)f5 or Ndf5; R(b) ×b4 or Rb×b4. If both Knights or both Rooks stand on the *same file* the number of the rank on which the piece stood is named, like this: N(3)d4; R(2)×c6.

If there are doubled pawns on the same file, the more advanced pawn takes the name of the file, while the more backward is called by the square it stands on, even if it was the original pawn on the file.

Four games to play over

Here is a short game for you to practise on. Set up your board and play it over. It was played over 300 years ago by a brilliant Italian player called Greco. It is a perfect example of what can happen (in this case to Black) when you don't keep an eye on what your opponent is up to!

White	*Black*
1 d4	f5
2 Bg5	h3
3 Bf4	g5
4 Bg3	f4

Black hopes to trap and capture the enemy bishop; but White has other things in mind!

5 e3!

Now the bishop cannot be captured because of Qh5 mate.

5 ...	h5
6 Bd3	Rh6
7 Q×h5+	R×h5
8 Bg6 mate	

Now here is another for you. This sparkling game was played by the young American chess genius Paul Morphy in 1858. It was played in a box at the Paris Opera against the Duke of Brunswick and Count Isouard during a performance of Rossini's *Barber of Seville*. Morphy was White and more than a match for his noble opponents.

White	*Black*
1 e4	e5
2 Nf3	d6
3 d4	Bg4
4 d×e5	B×f3
5 Q×f3	d×e5
6 Bc4	Nf6
7 Qb3	Qe7
8 Nc3	c6
9 Bg5	b5
10 N×b5!	c×b5
11 B×b5+	N(b)d7
12 O–O–O	Rd8
13 R×d7!	R×d7
14 Rd1	Qe6
15 B×d7+	N×d7
16 Qb8+!	N×b8
17 Rd8 mate	

In 1851 the German player Adolf Anderssen played a game which chess lovers have christened "The Immortal". Here it is.

Anderssen	*Kieseritzky*
1 e4	e5
2 f4	e×f4
3 Bc4	Qh4+
4 Kf1	b5
5 B×b5	Nf6
6 Nf3	Qh6
7 d3	Nh5
8 Nh4	Qg5
9 Nf5	c6
10 g4	Nf6
11 Rg1	c×b5
12 h4	Qg6
13 h5	Qg5
14 Qf3	Ng8
15 B×f4	Qf6
16 Nc3	Bc5
17 Nd5	Q×b2
18 Bd6	B×g1
19 e5	Q×a1+
20 Ke2	Na6
21 N×g7+	Kd8
22 Qf6+	N×f6
23 Be7 mate	

In 1883 Johannes Zukertort and Joseph Blackburne played this game. Zukertort unexpectedly offers his Queen. If Blackburne accepts, a forced mate follows. He refuses the offer but does not escape!

Zukertort	*Blackburne*
1 c4	e6
2 e3	Nf6
3 Nf3	b6
4 Be2	Bb7
5 O–O	d5
6 d4	Bd6
7 Nc3	O–O
8 b3	N(b)d7
9 Bb2	Qe7
10 Nb5	Ne4
11 N×d6	c×d6
12 Nd2	N(d)f6
13 f3	N×d2
14 Q×d2	d×c4
15 B×c4	d5
16 Bd3	R(f)c8
17 R(a)e1	Rc7
18 e4	R(a)c8
19 e5	Ne8
20 f4	g6
21 Re3	f5
22 e×f5 e.p.	N×f6
23 f5	Ne4
24 B×e4	d×e4
25 f×g6	Rc2
26 g×h7+	Kh8
27 d5+	e5
28 Qb4!	R(8)c5
29 Rf8+	K×h7
30 Q×e4+	Kg7
31 B×e5+	K×f8
32 Bg7+	Kg8
33 Q×e7	Resigns

Answers

Page 8

A1/D1 Because the white B will capture the R for nothing.

A2/D2 Because the e3 square is no longer protected by the B, Black can safely play 1 … Ne3, attacking both the Q and R at the same time.

A3/D3 Yes. Play 1 h4. The N can then retreat to g5 where it is supported by the h-pawn.

A4/D4 There is nothing Black can do to save the situation. 1 … h6 is met by 2 Qg6, followed by 3 R×h6. If 1 … Re8 to make an escape for the K, then 2 N×g5, threatening 3 B×f7+. If 2 … Kf8, then 3 B×f7 Re7 4 Ne6+ R×e6 5 B×e6, winning a R and 2 Ps for a N.

A5/D5 By playing 2 … Qd4+ and attacking the unprotected R on a1. If 2 Be3, then 2 … R×e3.

A6/D6 1 Be7! The B attacks Black's R on d8 *and* the white R on b1 is attacking the Q. Black must lose material here.

A7/D7 Because 1 b4 traps the N. Black should have played Nd4, forcing the move 1 Qd3 to defend the N and P on b3. Note that 1 Qc3 is no good because of 2 … Ne2+, winning the Q!

A8/D8 By playing 1 … b6. The B is under attack from the Q and cannot escape. 2 B×b6 Q×b6, loses a B for 2 pawns – not good for White. If Qa4 to defend the B, then 2 … Nc5 drives the Q off the a-file.

Page 10

A1/D1 1 Nf7, attacking both rooks.

A2/D2 By playing 1 … Bb5.

A3/D3 Because his K is too far away from the black P to stop it queening.

A4/D4 No. White can move either P and will queen one of them. Set up the position and try it for yourself.

A5/D5 Certainly not 1 R×c2, because of 1 … Re1 mate. So White must play 1 Rg1, and Black has won a piece for nothing.

A6/D6 No. It is a draw, for the simple reason that the B cannot guard the queening square. So long as the black K retreats to h8, the P cannot queen. Note however that this draw is only possible with an a- or h-pawn.

Pages 12/13

A1/D1 White overlooked that his R was now under attack from Black's B. White should have played 1 g3, followed by 2 Kg2, when he would capture the B for a P.

A2/D2 1 B×e5 is no use because the B will be captured by Black's N. The move White made is a bad one because it exposes his Q to an attack from a B. Equally bad moves are (1) to move the light-squared B, when the Q comes under attack from the R, and (2) to move the N, when White's R is exposed to a B attack. White's best move is to play 1 Qe2. This still defends the B on d3 and the e-pawn, which is attacked by a B. Now if Black were to play 1 … e4, the white B is free to capture it.

A3/D3 No, for this would allow the unprotected N to be captured by the R. Far better to play 1 Ne3, which brings the N out of danger *and* gives additional protection to the c-pawn.

A4/D4 White overlooked the fact that to play e5 *after* Black had played c5, opened up the long diagonal and allowed Black to capture the R with his B.

A5/D5 By White playing 1 d4 he is taking away his one and only guard on the e4 square. This would allow Black to play 1 … Ne4 attacking two major pieces (Q and R), winning the exchange next move. White has a choice of moves: Rf2, Kh1, Kh2 and Qf2. 1 Kh1 is probably the safest move, so long as White keeps his eye on Black's N. He must not let the N move via h5, to g3, which attacks both K and R, again winning the exchange.

A6/D6 No. After White's last move Black's B at e7 can no longer defend his Q because the B is "pinned" against his K. Therefore if 1 … d×c4, then 2 Q×d8 mate!

Pages 14/15

A1/D1 The a-pawn is now attacked by the B. Two possible moves for Black are 1 … a6 and 1 … b6.

A2/D2 Black's N move has unmasked an attack on White's unprotected N. What is more, the white N cannot move away because of the attack on the R. So, White must protect the N either with the Q or B on d2. 1 Qd2 gives the rooks more freedom along the back rank.

A3/D3 The reason for 1 Bf1 is to move to b5 next and attack the Q, and then the R if the Q moves away. So long as Black sees the intended move, it is very simple to stop it. Either move the Q or R, or play 1 … a6.

A4/D4 Black's last move has opened the long diagonal for his B. He is wanting to play 1 … Bd4 attacking a R which cannot move because of check to the white K. White's reply must be either a K move, then if the R is attacked it can safely move away, or a R move, and if the K is checked by the B, it moves out of check. Note that 1 c3 cannot be played, for the P is needed to protect the B.

A5/D5 The very fact that Black has left his a-pawn unprotected, should alert White to danger. But where can the B move to which will cause White problems? The answer is nowhere, and so it becomes clear that the reason for Black's move is to guard the h2 square and so prevent the K from escaping. Black threatens 2 … Re1 mate! White has four possible moves. 1 Kf1 which is perhaps best; 1 g3; and two other moves, 1 f3 and 1 Rc1 that are not good, the first one because it opens up dark squares for the enemy B (especially the g3 square), and the other because the R is needed on the 2nd rank, to protect the a- and f-pawns, and prevent Black from playing Re2.

A6/D6 The answer is White can ignore the threat to his R because his P is near to queening and it cannot be stopped. White plays 1 e7 N×h3 2 e8 = Q+ and wins with no trouble.

A7/D7 The one reasonable move for Black is 1 … d5 cutting off the B attack on f7.

A8/D8 Black *can* ignore the attack on his a-pawn (try it and see). But, he cannot press on with his attack on the c-pawn because of 1 … d4 2 Q×h7 mate!

Page 20

A1/D2 If 1 … Kg8, then 2 Qb3+. The R can interpose, then 3 Q×d5 mate. If 1 … h×g6, then 2 h×g6 dis ch Kg8 3 Qb3+ Kf8 4 Qf7 mate. If instead of 2 … Kg8 Black gives up his Q for R and N it does not help him, e.g. 2 … Qh6 3 R×h+ g×h6 4 Re7, threatening 5 Rh7+ Kg8 6 Qb3+ Kf8 7 Qf7 mate.

A2/D3 (How?) 1 … Q×h2 mate. (Why?) Because of the B on b7. (How?) 1 … Q×h2 mate! But White is not quite lost. He can play 1 Nf1, defending the h-pawn a second time.

A3/D4 White plays 1 b3.

A4/D5 By playing 1 c4. Note that although the N is trapped it will not be so easy to capture it as in previous example.

A5/D6 First, of course, Black must move the rook which is under attack from the N. A useful outpost for Black's N is g3 supported later, perhaps, by a P at h4.

Page 23

A1/D6 Yes, thanks to his extra P on the Q-side: 1 … a5 2 b×a5 (otherwise the a-pawn runs on to queen), Kb7 3 Kf2 Ka6. Now finish the game for Black yourself.

A2/D8 The difference is that a B, when attacked, can move well away and yet still protect the P, e.g. 1 … Ka5 2 Bc6 Kb6 3 Bb5 a6 4 Be8. Now the white K can move towards the enemy P and capture it and White can then go on to queen his P.

Page 24

A1/D2 The move is 1 … e4 attacking the N, *and* uncovering an attack on the a-rook from the B. There is no way

White can avoid losing material. He must keep his R and so 2 c3 seems best. 2 … e×f3 3 B×f3. White has lost a N for a P, a very bad start to the game.
A2/D3 Black cannot capture the B with the a-pawn because of 4 R×a8! So it is *White* who wins a P and not Black!
A3/D4 No. If Black plays 1 … g6, which wards off the immediate threat of mate (R×g7, etc), he is safe enough. In fact Black is a P to the good, and this may give him the advantage later in the game. To be a single move ahead often means the difference between losing and winning!

Page 26
A1/D1 If 1 Q×f2 Nd3+ wins the Q for a N and B. If 1 K×f2, then N×e4+ also winning the Q. Note that if 4 Q×c5, then 4 … Nd3+ again wins the Q. Generally speaking when a Q is brought out early to capture a P, and it is then attacked, it is better to retreat the Q to its starting square. White would have been better to play 2 Qd1 giving up the e-pawn.
A2/D2 After 1 … Qa6 (the only square!) White plays 1 Nd6, attacking both rooks.
A3/D5 No! 1 R×a3 Q×a3 2 Q×b7, and Black has lost his B for nothing. He should have moved his B to f8 (to stop the back-rank mate).

Pages 28/29
A1/D3 Here is one possible solution for each position. **K + Q v K.** 1 Qe4 Kc7 2 Qe6 Kc8 3 Qf7 Kd8 4 Ke3 Kc8 5 Kd4 Kb8 6 Kc5 Kc8 7 Kc6 Kb8 8 Qb7 mate.
K + R v K. 1 Ke3 Kd5 2 Kf4 Kd4 3 Rd1+, forcing the K to another file. 3 … Kc3 4 Ke4 Kc2 5 Rd3, preventing the K from escaping to the centre of the board. 5 … Kb2 6 Kd4 Kc2 7 Kc4 Kb2 8 Rc3 further limiting the King's movements. 8 … Ka2 9 Kb4 Kb2 10 Rc8 Ka2 11 Kc3 Kb1 12 Ra8. The vital move, for it forces the enemy K to come opposite your K. 12 … Kc1 13 Ra1 mate. This of course is only one possible sequence of moves, but the same principles apply no matter which moves Black makes. Note how unnecessary it is to check continuously.

A2/D8 Space does not allow us to demonstrate a solution, which, for a B and N may take anything up to 34 moves. Two bishops should be able to mate within 18 moves.

Pages 30/31
A1/D1 Yes. It must be the R, because the Q must stay on the 3rd rank to protect the N, under attack from Black's R.
A2/D2 Yes, thanks to the fact that both the white pieces under attack are also attacking the same piece (Black's N). Correct play is 1 R×f5 R×d3. If 1 … B×f5, then 2 B×f5, and White is better off.
A3/D3 White's trap is 1 … Q×d5 2 Rc5, and there is no way that Black can save his Q *and* his B. The B is lost. Black must play 1 … e×d5 and this isolates his P (the same as White's d-pawn is isolated).
A4/D4 1 … Bd7, because it blocks the only escape square for the black K. White plays 2 Qh5 mate!
A5/D5 The point to note here is that the black B is needed to defend his N, which is attacked twice. When White plays his next move, 2 b5, the B must flee to e8 and then 3 Q×e4. Black must prepare for this by playing 1 … b6. Now the B can retreat to b7 or a8 and still defend the N. Note that 1 … Q×e3 2 R×e3 doesn't solve the problem.
A6/D6 First 1 Nc4 attacking a R; 1 … R(a)a7, then 2 Nd6+. After the K moves White captures a R for his N, and material is equal again.
A7/D7 The difference in these two positions is that White is protecting his two backward pawns with his R on e2, while Black is not. White plays 1 Rc7 attacking the b-pawn. If 1 … R(a)b8 then 2 R(e)e7 threatening mate in two if the R on f8 doesn't move (3 R×h7+ Kg8 4 R(c)g7 mate). If Black tries "tit for tat" and plays 2 … Rf2, then white continues 3 R×h7+ Kg8 4 a4 Rb2 5 R×b7, White is two pawns up and is defending his b-pawn. If Black's first move is 1 … R(a)c8 then 2 R×b7 and White is one P up.
A8/D8 No. If 1 … R×a3, then 2 Kb2 and the R is lost. So all White must do is to defend his e-pawn with his R: 1 Re2, and both pawns are safe.
A9/D9 1 R×f7+. It is very important that White captures the N this way. First it is a check, forcing a K move, and establishing his R on the 7th rank. But equally important, the B must be able to guard the queening square (g8). 1 … Kg8 2 R×c7 Rb8 (it makes no difference if the B moves to safety); 3 Bb3+ Kf8 (not 3 … Kh8 4 g7+ Kh7 5 g8=Q dbl ch, mate) 4 g7+ Ke8 5 g8=Q mate. Play is exactly the same if Black's first move is 1 … Ke8.
A10/D10 No, not necessarily, because Black's weak, backward g-pawn can be blocked and captured. 1 Be7+ Kd7 2 Bg5 Bc2 3 Kf7 Bd1 4 K×g6 B×e2 5 K×f5 and there is a chance of White winning with his extra P.
A11/D11 The obvious move is 1 Rd2 but this loses to 1 … Qc4+ 2 Kd1 Kb6 3 Rc2 Q×c2+ 4 K×c2 K×c7. The next try is 1 Kc3, but this too loses: 1… Qe5+ 2 K moves Q×c7, and White's last hope has gone. We are left with the unexpected move, 1 Kc1! Black soon sees that to keep checking gets him nowhere, e.g. 1 … Qe1+ 2 Kc2 Qe2+ 3 Kc1 etc., and so he is obliged to play 1 … Q×d3 2 c8=Q+. Black still has the advantage of two pawns, one a passed P.

Nevertheless there is at least a faint hope of a draw for White, with a Q instead of a R.
A12/D12 If you found this one you are well on the way to becoming a good player. If you didn't, don't give up hope. Black's well-thought-out surprise move is 1 … Nf3+! If either the R or P takes the N, then 2 … B×d4+ (destroying the defender of the Q) 3 c×d4 Q×b5, and White would resign immediately. If, however, White saw what was coming and played 2 Kh1, then 2 … N×d4. Black has won a N for nothing, for if 3 Q×c6 N×c6; and if the Q moves away, the N moves to safety.

Pages 32/33
A1/D3 (A) No, because it allows White a nice fork: 1 Na6+. After the K moves White exchanges his N for the R, relying on his extra P to win him the game.
A2/D4 (B) Neither side. White, of course, plays 1 Bh4 moving his B from danger and still protecting his N. The postion is probably drawn anyway, but Black made sure by exchanging his R for the two minor pieces: 1 … R×f6 2 B×f6, K×f6.
A3/D11 White takes the P! 1 B×f6 g×f6 2 N× f6+, and wins the Q. Black has lost a Q and two pawns for a B and should resign!
A4/D12 After White's R moves to safety, Black plays 1 … Ne3+, forking K and B. This shows the need to watch the N and to see where it can go next move and the next move after that.

Page 35
A1/D1 No. Black's Q is protected. The N is merely shielding his Q from an immediate exchange of queens, and can move away at any time depending on whether Black is willing to exchange queens. Note however that if the d1 square were occupied by a R instead of the Q, then of course the N would be pinned, because the R is a lesser piece than the Q.
A2/D2 White should lose anyway with a N down and an enemy P on the 2nd rank. But if he doesn't move his R he will lose it as well as the N, e.g. 1 b4 h×g2+ 2 R×g2, and now not 2 … B×g2 3 K×g2 (although that would win too), but 2 … Rg7! 3 Kg1 R×g2+ etc.
A3/D4 By bringing his R on to a file between the e-file and his K. This avoids a check if White does play Re8: 1 … Rf8 (this leaves a square for his K), 2 Re8 Kg8 (unpinning the N), and Black has avoided the mate.
A4/D5 White's B is pinning the N on Black's Q. But Black has to be considerably more careful in how he deals with this pin. The reason is the other "hidden" pin, which White has up his sleeve. For example it is no use Black moving his Q or driving away the B with h6, because White simply plays B×f6 or B×h6, thanks to the white R pinning the g-pawn. Black's best plan is to move his K away from the "hidden" pin by playing Kh8, and then deal with the bishop's pin later. The K move also allows his R to move to g8 to give added support to the g-pawn. And this in turn (once the Q has moved) gives a square for his N to give still more protection to the vital g-pawn.

A5/D7 When Black plays 1 … Ne4, not only does the white B on g5 come under attack from three pieces, but the big difference is that the N also attacks the R on c3. If the R moves away then Black wins a piece with 2 … N×g5 3 N×g5 B×g5. And if 2 B×e7 N×c3 3 B×d8 N×d1 4 R×d1 R(a)×d8; and White has lost the exchange.
A6/D8 By playing 1 … Bc3, attacking White's rooks. White must lose the exchange.

Pages 36/37
A1 Queen, Rook, or Bishop.
A2/D8 Yes. The simplest way is to move the second B from the back rank, which allows the Q to guard the g8 square, so, after 2 Bb6, Be7. If White carries on with his original plan, then after 3 Ng5, Black plays 3 … R×e1 , and White can put into operation a perpetual check: 4 Nf7+ Kg8 5 Nh6 dbl ch Kh8, etc.

Page 39
A1/D2 1 … R(e)×e1 2 R×e1 Q×e1+ 3 Kc2 Rd2+ 4 Kc3 Re2 dis ch 5 Kd3 Qd2 mate.
A2/D6 White plays 1 R×e6+! f×e6 2 Qh5 mate. If Black had played 1 … Be7, then 2 N×d6+ Kf8 3 Bh6+ Kg8 4 Qg4+ Bg5 5 Re8+ Q×e8 6 Q×g5 mate.

Page 41
A1/D5 (*a*) 1 Re6 f×e6 2 f6. If 2 … g×f6 3 Q×h7+ Kf8 4 Bh6 mate. If 2 … g6 3 B×g6 h×g6 4 Q×g6+ Kf8 5 Qg7 mate *or* 3 … B×g2+ 4 K×g2 Qc6+ 5 Rf3 Qd7 6 f7+ Kf8 7 Qh6+ Ke7 8 Bg5 mate.
A2/D5 (*b*) If 5 … g×f6 , then 6 Bh6+, Qg7 7 Q×g7 mate.

Page 42
A1/D1 3 … Kg7 4 Qf6+ Kg8 5 Rc8 mate. If 3 … Kf7; then 4 Rf6+ Kg7 5 Qf8 mate. If 2 … Qg7; then 3 Q×d8+ Qg8 4 Qf6+ Qg7 5 Rc8 mate.
A2/D3 (*a*) If 1 … Kg8; then 2 Q×g7 mate.
A3/D3 (*b*) For the same reason: 3 … Q×e8 4 Q×g7 mate.

Page 44
A1/D4 Yes. Black's mistake was taking the R. If instead, Black had played 3 … Nc5, forcing the white Q to c2 (4. Qc2) in order to protect the R on f5, then Black could play 4 … Re8, and if 5 Rf1, Qe7, and all is well.

Pages 46/47
A1/D2 *White to play* 1 Kc3 Kf6 2 g4, protecting the attacked pawn, 2 … Kg5 3 K×c4 a5 4 Kb5, and the remaining black P is snapped up next move. It is easy to see that the two isolated pawns are no match for White's K.
Now see what happens if Black captures a P.
Black to play 1 … Kf6 2 g4 Kg5 3 Kc3 K×g4 4 f6 Kg5 5 f7 Kg6 6 f8 = Q and White wins easily. If Black tries to queen a pawn he loses: 1 … a5 2 Kc3 a4 3 K×c4 a3 4 Kb3, and the P is lost. White's K is then free to help one of his pawns to queen.
A2/D3 (**A**) 1 … a6 2 Ba4, now if 2 … Ka5, White's P will go on to queen. After Black moves, White brings up his K to assist his P through.
(**B**) All Black needs to do is to play h5, driving the N away, and then K×f6 . If the N were placed on e4, it could not be attacked at all, for if the K moved to f5 the white P would push on and queen. So the white K deals with the black P and once that is captured can then help his P to queen.
A3/*Game* Black loses his Q by 11 … d×e6 12 Q×d8, or if 11 … Kg8 12 N×d8. But if 11 … K×e6; then, 12 Qd5+ Kf5 13 g4+ K×g4 14 Rg1+. Black has four squares for his K: 14 … Kf5 15 Rg5 mate/14 … Kh5 15 Qd1+ Kh4 16 Qg4 mate/14 … Kh3 15 Qg2+ Kh4 16 Qg4 mate/ 14 … Kh4 15 Bg5+ Kh5 16 Qd1+ with mate next move, or15 … Kh3 16 Qg2 mate.

Page 49
A1/D1 Here is a position that you can puzzle over for hours. It is included because the action is confined to one quarter of the board and enables you to practise using the men to the best advantage. Black's strength, of course, is his easy access to the h-file with his Q, and his control of the dark squares. We think that White has left it too late to ward off Black's strong mating attack. But if you can see a way out for White please do write to us c/o Collins, the Publishers.
A2/D7 This demonstrates correct King play. From the diagram 1 Kb4 Ke4 2 Ka5! Ke5. (Not 2 … Kd4 because of 3 Kb5, and now if the black K moves to either e4 or e5, where he is no longer attacking the c-pawn, White plays 4 Kc6 and Black is lost. And if he moves his K to either d3 or c3, then White can push on his pawns to queen one of them.) 3 Ka6 Kd6 4 Kb7 Kd7. (If 4 … Kc5, then 5 K×c7 K×b4 6 d6 and queens.) 5 c5 Kd8 6 P move. If either P moves White can win the game. But let us look at both P moves. One of them is a perfect example of chess at its best – neat in its effect and the surest and shortest way to victory. The other one is poor chess (even though it may still win), clumsy, and in fact if White played poorly again, the game could end up in a draw. The correct move is 6 c6, driving the K away from the protection of his P. The poor move is 6 d6 c×d6 7 c6 and queens before Black can. Note, however, that if 6 … c×d6 7 c×d6 Kd7, it is a draw!
A3/D9 It is no use White playing 1 c7 because of 1 … B×c7 2 B×c7, and it is not possible for White to save either P for queening. So White employs the simple pin tactic, 1 Bg5! If 1 … B×g5, then 2 c7 and queens next move. Any other move and White exchanges bishops leaving his c-pawn free to queen.
A4/D10 If White cannot queen the c-pawn then Black will certainly queen one of his pawns. White must drive the B away from guarding the c7 square as quickly as possible. So 1 Nd6 K×h3 2 Nc4, and the B is either lost or White's c-pawn goes on to queen.

Page 51
A1/D2 This is an example of how a K can play a vital role, even in the middle game. White plays 1 Kg2 and this simple move stops the mighty Q from carrying out her plan.
A2/D3 Black tries blocking White's e-pawn: 1 … Kc7 2 Kf5 Kd7 3 Kf6 Ke8 4 e6 a5. So, thinks White, that's Black's game – lure my K over to one side of the board and then queen a P on the other. But surely it doesn't work? 5 Ke5 a4 6 Kd4 a3 7 Kc3 a2 8 Kb2. Black has it all worked out, and decides that is far enough for his a-pawn! 8 … Ke7 9 K×a2 K×e6 10 Kb2 Ke5 11 Kc2 Ke4 12 Kd2 Kf3 13 Kd3 K×g3 14 Ke3 Kh3 15 Kf2, but it is not good enough. Black shepherds his P home to queen.
A3/D4 (**A**) *Black to move.* (*a*) 1 … Kb7 2 Kd6 Kc8. Now White must keep the opposition by placing his K opposite the enemy K. 3 Kc6. Whichever side Black moves his K, White moves his K the other way: 3 … Kb8 4 Kd7 (guarding the queening square) Kb7 5 c5 Kb8 6 c6, and queens in two more moves.
(*b*) 1 … Kc8 2 Kd6 Kd8 3 c5 Kc8 4 Kc6 Kd8 5 Kb7 Kd7 6 c6+, etc.
White to move. Whichever way White moves his K, Black must keep his K opposite it. 1 Kd5 Kd7 2 Kc5 Kc7 3 Kb5 Kb7 4 c5 Kc7 5 Kb4 Kb7 6 Kb5 Kc7. There is nothing White can do to promote his P and it is a draw, e.g. 7 c6 Kc8 8 Kb6 Kb8 9 c7+ Kc8 10 Kc6, drawing.
(**B**) When there is a square between K and P it does not matter that White has to move. He plays 1 g4 and that is now exactly the same position as (**A**) with Black to move. White wins.
A4/D6 (**A**) The only way that White can win here is if the black K moves two files away from the P. But as there is no need for this, we can say that this position is a draw no matter who moves. Here is just one variation, with Black to move. 1 … Kc7 2 Ka5 Kb7 3 b6 Kb8 4 Ka6 Ka8 5 b7+ Kb8 6 Kb6, drawing.
(**B**) This is similar to the previous example. It doesn't matter who moves, it is a draw: 1 … Kg8 2 Kg6 Kh8 3 h7, stalemate.

Page 52/53
A1/D1 A good reply for Black is 1 … Nf6 for three reasons: it, allows another piece (R) to support the B; it attacks the N which, if Black does the exchanging, may isolate a white P; and it opens up the possibility of a good discovered attack. If White plays 2 Bd3 then 2 … N×e4 3 f×e4. It has to be the P that takes, as

you will see by the next variation. If White, not wanting to exchange the N, moves it to f2 or g5, then a nice discovered attack: 2 ... B×h2+ 3 K×h2 R×d1 4 R(f)×d1, and Black has come out on top. If 2 N×f6 then Black plays the same moves as before – 2 ... B×h2+, etc. White will probably decide that 2 N×d6 is best. 2 ... R×d6; and the Q moves. So far as Black is concerned this is a fair exchange and his N is on a better square than it was.

A2/D2 after 1 f6, Black can do one of three things: play 1 ... g6; 1 ... g×f6; or move another man altogether. White's plan had to allow for any one of these three possibilities.

(1) **1 ... g6** is best for White! 2 Qh6, and next move 3 Qg7 mate.

(2) **1 ... g×f6** 2 Bh4. The plan here is 3 B×f6 and 4 Qg5 mate. Black has a few possible moves but none of them stops the mate except by losing valuable material. The moves are: 2 ... Ne7; 2 ... R(a)e8; 2 ... Q×d4; 2 ... N×d4; 2 ... R(f)c8. Try them for yourself.

(3) **1 ... h6.** If Black doesn't play either (1) or (2) then he must prevent 2. Qg5. After 1 ... h6. White has to alter his tactics: 2 Be3 Kh7 3 f×g7 Rg8 4 R×f7. White is now a pawn up and he is threatening 5 Qf2 and Qf5 mate. If 4 ... R×g7 5 Qf2 R×f7 6 Q×f7+ Kh8 7 B×h6 Rg8 8 Qh5 Rg7 (otherwise 9 Bf8 is mate) 9 Rf1 with a mating attack.

A3/D3 "I must drive the N away with my h-pawn, so 1 ... h5 2 Rf2 h4 3 Nf1. Now 3 ... Nd4 looks good because of 4 ... B×g2. If 4 Ne3 to guard g2, then I can play 4 ... Qh5, threatening 5 ... Ne2+ or even 5 ... Rg3! 6 h×g3 followed by 7 ... Qh2+, with a strong attack. And if 4 B×d4, then 4 ... B×g2 5 Ne3 Bf3 dis ch 6 Ng2 B×g2 7 Rd2 Bf3 dis ch 8 Rg2 B×g2 should lead to mate.

A4/D4 White had thought of 1 d4, which would destroy the hole if Black responded by 1 ... e×d4 2 R×d4; but Black need not capture. Then if 2 d×e5 f×e5, the problem hasn't really been solved, although Black's e-pawn is isolated and therefore weaker; and there is still the question of the B which is hampering the movement of White's rooks. So White plays 1 Nd5, forcing the Q to move, and then 2 N×b4.

A5/D5 Black's *strengths* are very few. A strong control of the d5 square, and the ability to drive away the N nuisance with b6, thus opening up another route for his B. Black's overall *weakness* is the immobility of his major pieces and B. There is a hole on b6 but it is likely that all White's efforts will be directed to the K side. Black has little scope for making a plan of attack and his moves will be dictated largely by White's moves.

White's Plan. White plays 1 Qg3, with threat of 2 B×h6 and 3 Q×g7 mate. If (*a*) 1 ... g5, then 2 B×g5 h×g5 3 Q×g5 + Kh8 4 Qh6+ Kg8 5 Re5, threatening 6 Rg5 mate is very strong. If (*b*) 1 ... N (either) e8, then 2 B×h6, wins a P for a start. If (*c*) 1 ... Nh5, then 2 Qg6! Qh4 3 Re4 Be6? 4 R×h4 f×g6 5 N×e6 N×e6 6 B×e6+ and wins a piece. If (*d*) 1 ... Kh7 2 Qh4, threatening 3 Bc2+ Kg8 4 B×h6 g×h6 5 Q×h6, followed by 6 Re5 and 7 Rg5 or h5 depending on Black's last move. There are lots of other possible moves, but White's plan and his own analysis of Black's possible moves, showed him that at least he will come ooout of it with advantage, and so he played 1 Qg3.

A6/D6 One way is 1 c4 d×c4 2 Ne4. If 2 ... c×b3 3 N×g3 f×g3 4 R×f7 R×f7 5 Qc8+, with mate to follow. Or 3 ... b×a2 4 R×f4 Qb1 5 R×f7 R×f7 6 Qc8+! Another possibility is 1 ... d×c4 2 Q×c4 Q×c4 3 b×c4, when White can concentrate on his two united central pawns and there is not the same necessity to dislodge Black's B. If Black doesn't exchange queens but plays, say, 2 ... Qf5 to prevent 3 Ne4, then 3 d5, and if 3 ... Rc8 4 Qe4 Qf6? 5 R×g3 f×g3 6 R×f6 R×f6 7 Qe1, and White, threatening 8 Q×g3 should win with his more powerful army.

A7/D7 White's N and g-pawn are both under attack from the Q. There are four moves which Black had to consider: 1 N×f7; 1 Ng4; 1 B×f7+; and 1 f4.

(*a*) 1 N×f7 Q×g2 2 Rf1 Q×e4+ 3 Be2 Nf6 mate – a kind of smothered mate.

(*b*) 1 Ng4 d5, and Black gains a little material and a much better developed position, e.g. 2 B×d5 B×g4 3 f3 Bc8 4 g3 c6 5 Bc4, etc. Black has won a N for two pawns.

(*c*) 1 B×f7+ Ke7; now it is two pieces and a P en prise. Having stopped Black from castling, White's best hope may be to castle and give up the N. Any other move makes White's position worse.

(*d*) 1 f4 Q×g2 2 Rf1 Q×e4+ 3 Kf2 (3 Be2 loses the Q to 3 ... N×c2+ 4 Q×c2 Q×c2!) Nf5 dis ch, and White must lose a lot of material to avoid an immediate mate.

Page 54

A1/D1 The success of White's plan depends on the black K being confined to two files only. White also sees that the black N has few moves open to it. So 1 Rg3+ (not 1 Rh3 right away because Black can capture the R: 1 ... R×h3 2 K×h3 h1=Q+! And not 1 Rd1 because of 1 ... Rh5 2 Rh1 R×f5 3 R×h2 R×f4) 1 ... Kh7 2 Rh3+ Kg7 3 R×h8 K×h8 4 K×h2 Kg7 5 Kg2. White's plan is to move his K across to the Q side and free his a-pawn for queening. 5 ... Nd2, a nice little trap for White! White wants to play 6 Kf2 but he sees the trap (6 Kf2 Ne4+ 7 Ke3 N×c5 8 b×c5, and the black K can move via f8 to stop the P from queening). So this is a good example of a player having to adjust his plan to suit a new position. Therefore 6 Be7 Ne4 7 Kf3 Nd2+ 8 Ke3 Nf1+ 9 Kd4 Ng3 10 Kd5 (not 10 Kc5, for after 10 ... N×f5 the B would be forced to move to d8 and allow the black K to move to f8) 10 ... N×f5 11 Bc5 Kg6 12 Kc6 Ng3 13 Kb6, etc.

A2/D2 One lesson to learn from this position is "Never panic", no matter how grim the situation. If you lose, you lose, but quite often, hidden away somewhere, is a move that can save the situation. Black's weak spot is his unprotected d-pawn, which is on the same diagonal as his badly placed K. In fact 1 Q×d4 nearly comes off because of mate next move (2 Nf7 dbl ch mate), but Black's attack saves him: 1 ... Nh3+ 2 Kf1 f×g2+ 3 Ke2 Re8 (pinning the N) 4 Kd3 Kg8, and Black has freed himself. However White thought out another plan based on the Q×d4 idea: 1 Ng6+! h×g6 (1 ... R×g6 is not good because of 2 Q×d4+ and if either R or Q interposes then Re8 is mate. And if 2 ... Kg8, then 3 Qd8+ Kg7 4 Re7+ Q×e7 5 Q×e7+ and the outcome is uncertain.) 2 Q×d4+ Qg7 3 Q×h4+ Qh7 4 Q×g5 the position is even again.

A3/D3 White planned: 1 Nh6+ Kh8 2 Q×e5! Q×e5 3 Nf7+ – the point of the plan, because if 3 ... R×f7, the white R mates on a8. Black must content himself with 3 ... Kg8 4 N×e5 and he has lost a piece for nothing.

A4/D4 After 1 g4, it doesn't matter what move Black makes – he cannot avoid mate. White threatens 2 Qh8+ Kg6 3 Qg8+ Bg7 4 Q×g7 mate. If Black plays 1 ... h5, then 2 Qh8+ Kg6 3 Q×h5 mate. But what difference can it possibly make if White plays first 1 Qh8+ and then 2 g4? Well, he soon found out: 2 ... Q×h2+! K×h2 3 Bd6+ 4 K moves R×h8 and it is Black who is winning!

A5/D5 2 R×d5! Q×d5 3 Q×e7+ Kg8 3 Q×f6 and now White has two more threats: 4 Qg7 mate; and if 3 ... Rh7; the other threat of 4 Ne7+ winning the Q. What a delightful finish for a boy of 12 years!

A6/D6 This is a particularly interesting theme of discovered check and one well worth remembering. The key move is 1 Bf6! Q×h5 2 R×g7+ Kh8 3 R×f7 dis ch Kg8 4 Rg7+ Kh8 5 R×b7 dis ch Kg8 6 Rg7+ Kh8 7 Rg5 dis ch Kh7 8 R×h5 White has won a B and two Ps for nothing.

A7/D7 The N protects the R and the K guards the N, so how can Black force the K away? 1 ... h5+ doesn't work because of 2 Kg5. So there must be a preparatory move: 1 ... f6 2 R×e4, and now 2 ... h5+ and the K cannot move to g5. 3 K×h5 (If Kh4, then 3 ... Q×h2 mate) Q×f5+ 4 Kh4 Q×e4+, and White resigns.

A8/D8 White's plan succeeded because each of Black's moves were forced: 1 Qg7+ Q×g7 2 f×g7+ Kg8. Now the fork: 3 Ne7+ K×g7 4 N×c8, and Black resigned being a R down, with his own R temporarily out of action. Note that 4 R×c8 R×c8 5 N×c8 would also win easily.

A9/D9 1 R×g5+ Kf7 (1 ... f×g5 lets White win with 2 Q×f8 mate) 2 R×f6+ K×f6 3 Q×f8+ K×g5 4 h4+ Resigns. If 4 ... K×h4 (or Kg4) 5 Qf4 mate, and if 4 ... Kg6 5 Nf4 mate.

A10/D10 It would be a simple matter to win back the piece with 2 R×g5 dis ch, but that was too slow for Fischer. He played 2 Re5 dis ch, forcing 2 ... Kf8. 3 R×e8+, and Black resigned, because after 3 ... K×e8 4 Qe6+ Kf8 5 Qc8+ and mate follows.

A11/D11 4 Nf6, opening up the long diagonal for his Q.

4 … Rh1. Black carries on with his plan. 5 Qb7 (threatening Q×h7 mate), Ng7; 6 Qf7. Black sees the mate now (Qf8) but too late. He tries for a perpetual check with 6 … Rg1+. White, however, doesn't fall for 7 B×g1 for then 7 … Q×g1 and it really would be a perpetual check. Instead White puts his K on a square where he cannot be attacked 7 Kf3, and the game is over.

A12/D12 The six Black moves are 1 … f×g5; 1 … Ne7; 1 … Qe7; 1 … d6; 1 … Bg7; and 1 … Ke7. Here are White's plans:

(1) **1 … f×g5** 2 Qh5+ Ke7 3 B×g5+ Kd6 4 B×d8 N×d8 5 Qe5 mate

(2) **1 … Ne7**, with the idea of 2 … Ng6 when the Q checks on h5. But all White need do now is play 2 Ne6 to win the Q for a N.

(3) **1 … Qe7** 2 Qh5+ Kd8 3 Nf7+ Ke8 4 N×h8 dis ch Kd8 5 Nf7+. White has won a R for nothing and can move his N to safety by means of another dis ch.

(4) **1 … d6** 2 Qh5+ Kd7 3 Nf7, forking Q and R. If 3 … Qe8, pinning N on Q, then 4 Qd5 Rg8 5 Ne5+ f×e5 6 Q×g8, and White has won a R for a N and P, and has devastated Black's K-side.

(5) **1 … Bg7** 2 Qh5+ Kf8 3 Qf7 mate

(6) **1 … Ke7** 2 Qh5 Qe8 3 Q×e8 K×e8 4 N×e4 , and White has won a P, has upset Black's position, and stopped him from castling.

Page 56

A1/D1 The white N stands on c3, and the white B on f4. The black Q stands on e7 and the black R on e8.

A2/D2 The white R stands on a1 and moves Rd1. The white pawn stands on d2 and moves d4. The white N stands on f3 and moves Ne5. The black N stands on b4 and moves Nc6. The black B stands on e7 and moves Bg5. The black P stands on a7 and moves a6.